SPANISH made FUN and EASY
For Ages 10 - Adult

Written by
Kathleen Fisher
and
Kathrane Wilcoxon

Fisher Hill   Huntington Beach   California

Copyright 1995, 2006 by Kathleen Fisher
Second Printing 1997
Third Printing 2003
All rights reserved.

Published by FISHER HILL
5267 Warner Avenue, #166
Huntington Beach, CA 92649-4079

Made in the U.S.A.

Publisher's Cataloging in Publication

Fisher, Kathleen S., 1952-
    Spanish made fun and easy : for ages 10-adult / by Kathleen Fisher and Kay Wilcoxon. --1st ed.
    p. cm.
    Includes bibliographical references and index.
      ISBN 1-878253-42-5

    1. Spanish language--Self instruction. 2. Spanish language--Textbooks for foreign speakers--English.   I. Wilcoxon, Kathrane, 1924- II. Title.

PC4112.5.F57 1995   468.2'421
                                                          QBI94-1490

Table of Contents

Introduction

This book was written for the beginning student; for the person who wants to brush up on Spanish; or for the Spanish speaker who wants to learn how to read and write Spanish. It is for ages ten to adult.

There are twelve lessons in the book. Each lesson deals with a common theme, i.e., Breakfast, Telling Time, etc. At the end of the book are two dictionaries: Spanish-English and English-Spanish.

Each lesson is divided into eight parts. First, there is a vocabulary list. Beginning Spanish is included as well as the vocabulary of the particular theme. The definite article is placed in front of each Spanish noun on the list, letting the student know whether it is a feminine or masculine noun. Then there is a conversation in order to use the vocabulary in a common situation. Next is a story related to the theme which reinforces the vocabulary and the conversation. The fourth page of each lesson is an exercise that requires choosing a word from the vocabulary list and then writing it in a sentence that is missing that word. The next three pages are a variety of activity pages. At the end of each lesson are the answers to the exercises.

It is recommended that the student do one lesson per week but the pupil can go through the book more rapidly if he or she so desires. The speed at which the student learns Spanish depends on the student. It would be useful to read the conversation and story out loud to gain smoothness.

Also, the student should listen to television in Spanish. In the beginning the pupil should listen to ads, cartoons, and news. It is very important to listen to and speak with Spanish speakers. This will help the student greatly. He or she will be able to practice Spanish and also improve his or her accent. No one is ever going to learn Spanish without practice. Children learn quickly to speak another language. The reason for this is that most children are not bothered by the mistakes they make in speaking. It is important to take advantage of every opportunity to speak.

Teacher's Guide

Each lesson includes the following pages. Below are activities and ideas for each page.

Vocabulary Page
• teacher, student helper, or tutor pronounces the Spanish words and the students repeat
• the words from the vocabulary list can be used for a weekly spelling test
• students write each word three times
• students write sentences or a story using the vocabulary words

Conversation Page
• teacher, student helper, or tutor reads the conversation in Spanish and the students repeat
• students read the conversation together each taking a different part

Story Page
• teacher, student helper, or tutor reads one sentence at a time and the students repeat
• students read the story quietly to themselves
• students act out the story putting in their own Spanish dialog

Fill in the Blank and other Activity Pages
• students do these pages on their own
• different students go up to the board to write the answers while the other students correct their work
• students check their work with the Answer Key

Puzzle Fun
At the end of the book are puzzles. Each puzzle uses the vocabulary words from two lessons. (The first WordSearch uses vocabulary words from Lessons 1 and 2.) These puzzles provide extra practice for the students.

Related Activities
• in small groups, students make up and put on short skits about the lesson's theme using Spanish dialog
• students draw, paint, or create pictures about the lesson's theme and then explain or discuss their pictures in Spanish
• students talk about their own personal experience as it relates to the lesson's theme
• students write about their own personal experience as it relates to the lesson's theme and then read their stories to the group

Spanish Pronunciation Guide

Spanish is a phonetic language. Most letters in the Spanish alphabet make one sound. Most words are spelled like they are pronounced.

The Spanish alphabet has 30 letters. The underlined letters are not in the English alphabet.

a b c <u>ch</u> d e f g h i j k l <u>ll</u> m n ñ o p q r <u>rr</u> s t u v w x y z

K and **W** are only found in words of foreign origin.

The following is a basic and beginning pronunciation guide. It does not included everything about Spanish pronunciation but enough to get you started.

Spanish Letter	Sound of the Spanish Letter
Vowels	
a	like the *a* in **fa**ther
e	like the *e* in b**e**d
i	like the *i* in pol**i**ce
o	like the *o* in **o**pen
u	like the *oo* in f**oo**d
Consonants	
b and v	makes the sound of *b* as in **b**ig; makes the sound of *v* as in **v**ein when *b* or *v* comes between two vowels
c before a, o , u	makes the sound of *c* as in **c**an
c before e, i	makes the sound of *c* as in **c**ircle

ch	makes the sound of *ch* as in **ch**urch
d	makes the sound of *d* as in **d**og; makes the sound of *th* as in **th**ey when the *d* falls between two vowels as in ciu**d**ad
f	makes the sound of *f* as in **F**rank
g before a, o, u	makes the sound of *g* as in **g**um
g before e, i	makes the sound of *h* as in **h**ello
h	is silent as in honest
j	makes the sound of *h* as in **h**ello
k	only used in words of foreign origin
l	similar to the English *l* as in **l**ook
ll	makes a sound of *ll* as in bi**ll**ion
m	similar to the English *m* as in **m**y
n	similar to the English *n* as in **n**ight
ñ	makes the sound of *n* as in onion
p	similar to the English *p* as in **p**ig
qu	similar to the sound of the English *k*
r	The Spanish *r* is not similar to the English *r*. It requires a single flip of the tongue tip against the roof of the mouth. If the *r* is at the beginning of a word or preceded by l, n, or s then the *r* makes a strongly trilled sound.
rr	trilled *r*

s	similar to the English *s*
t	similar to the *t* in **ton**
w	not used in words of Spanish origin
x	similar but not identical to the English *x*
y	makes the sound of *y* as in **sunny**
z	similar to the English *s* sound

Diphthongs

ai, ay	makes the sound of *i* as in **mice**
ei, ey	makes the sound of *ay* as in **lay**
oi, oy	makes the sound of *oy* as in **boy**
au	makes the sound of *ow* as in **cow**

Accent or Stress

The three rules below tell you where to stress or emphasize Spanish words.

1. Stress the last syllable of the word if it ends in any consonant except *n* or *s*.

2. When the last syllable ends in a vowel or *n* or *s* stress the next to the last syllable.

3. If the emphasis does no follow Rules 1 or 2, then an accent mark is used to show which syllable is stressed.

Lección 1 ¡Hola!
Lesson 1 Hello!

Lista de Vocabulario	Vocabulary List
1. ¡hola!	1. hello!
2. usted	2. you
3. el nombre	3. name
4. ¿dónde?	4. where?
5. gustar	5. to like
6. yo	6. I
7. sí	7. yes
8. no	8. no
9. por favor	9. please
10. gracias	10. thank you
11. el; la	11. the

Conversación

1. ¡Hola!

2. ¿Cómo está usted?

3. Estoy bien. Gracias.

4. ¿Cómo se llama usted?

5. Me llamo _____ .

6. ¿De dónde es usted?

7. Yo soy de _____ .

8. ¿Le gustan los Estados Unidos?

9. Sí, me gustan los Estados Unidos.

10. Adiós, hasta luego.

Conversation

1. Hello!

2. How are you?

3. I am fine. Thank you.

4. What is your name?

5. My name is ___ .

6. Where are you from?

7. I am from _____ .

8. Do you like the United States?

9. Yes, I like the United States.

10. Good-bye, see you later.

Historia

Dos Amigos

Me llamo María Ramirez. Soy de Guadalajara, México. Sí, me gustan los Estados Unidos.

Me llamo José Garcia. Soy de San Salvador, El Salvador. No, no me gustan los Estados Unidos.

Story

Two Friends

My name is Maria Ramirez. I am from Guadalajara, Mexico. Yes, I like the United States.

My name is Jose Garcia. I am from San Salvador, El Salvador. No, I do not like the United States.

Fill in the Blank

Fill in the blanks using the vocabulary words. Use each word once.

1. Mi _____ es María.

2. ¿Cómo está _____ ?

3. ¿De _____ es usted?

4. _____ soy de México.

5. ¿A usted le _____ los Estados Unidos?

6. _____ , me gustan los Estados Unidos.

7. No, _____ me gustan los Estados Unidos.

8. ¡_____! Me llamo José.

9. Me gusta _____ lección.

Matching

Match up the Spanish and English words.

1. _____please

2. _____no

3. _____thank you

4. _____where?

5. _____I

6. _____yes

7. _____hello!

8. _____to like

9. _____you

10. _____name

11. _____the

¡hola!
usted
nombre
¿dónde?
gustar
yo
sí
no
por favor
gracias
el; la

Alphabetical Order

Below is the Spanish alphabet. It has 30 letters. The underlined letters are not in the English alphabet.

a b c <u>ch</u> d e f g h i j k l <u>ll</u> m n <u>ñ</u> o p q r <u>rr</u> s t u v w x y z

Write the vocabulary words (at the right) in alphabetical order.

1. _____

2. _____

3. _____

4. _____

5. _____

6. _____

7. _____

8. _____

9. _____

10. _____

11. _____

12. _____

| hola |
| usted |
| nombre |
| dónde |
| gustar |
| yo |
| sí |
| no |
| por favor |
| gracias |
| el |
| la |

Punctuation

In Spanish, sentences that ask a question begin and end with a question mark. Example: ¿Cómo está usted?

Rewrite the following sentences putting in the correct punctuation marks and capitalizing where needed.

1. me llamo María

   Me llamo María.

2. a usted le gustan los estados unidos

3. sí, me gustan los estados unidos

4. de dónde es usted

5. yo soy de méxico

6. no, no me gustan los estados unidos

7. cómo se llama usted

8. me llamo josé

Answer Key

Fill in the Blank (page 4)

1. nombre
2. usted
3. dónde
4. Yo
5. gustan
6. Sí
7. no
8. Hola
9. la

Matching (page 5)

1. por favor
2. no
3. gracias
4. ¿dónde?
5. yo
6. sí
7. ¡hola!
8. gustar
9. usted
10. nombre
11. el; la

Alphabetical Order (page 6)

1. dónde
2. el
3. gracias
4. gustar
5. hola
6. la
7. no
8. nombre
9. por favor
10. sí
11. usted
12. yo

Punctuation (page 7)

1. Me llamo María.
2. ¿A usted le gustan los Estados Unidos?
3. Sí, me gustan los Estados Unidos.
4. ¿De dónde es usted?
5. Yo soy de México.
6. No, no me gustan los Estados Unidos.
7. ¿Cómo se llama usted?
8. Me llamo José.

Lección 2 El Hogar
Lesson 2 Home

Lista de Vocabulario	Vocabulary List
1. el muchacho	1. boy
2. la muchacha	2. girl
3. los niños	3. children
4. ¿cuál?	4. what?; which one?
5. en	5. in; on
6. la dirección	6. address
7. vivir	7. to live
8. el número	8. number
9. mi	9. my
10. tener	10. to have
11. el teléfono	11. telephone
12. y	12. and

Conversación

1. ¿Dónde vive usted?

2. Yo vivo en Los Angeles.

3. ¿Cuál es su dirección?

4. Mi dirección es __ .

5. ¿Cuál es su número de teléfono?

6. Mi número de teléfono es _____ .

7. ¿Cuántos niños tiene usted?

8. Yo tengo __ niños.

9. ¿Son muchachos o muchachas?

10. Yo tengo _____ muchachos y ____ muchachas.

Conversation

1. Where do you live?

2. I live in Los Angeles.

3. What is your address?

4. My address is ___ .

5. What is your telephone number?

6. My telephone number is _____ .

7. How many children do you have?

8. I have ___ children.

9. Are they boys or girls?

10. I have __ boys and _____ girls.

10

Historia

El Hogar

María vive en Los Angeles. Su dirección es 454 La Ciénaga. Su número de teléfono es 957-8251. María tiene 6 niños. Ella tiene 2 muchachos y 4 muchachas.

José vive en Long Beach. Su dirección es 567 Miramar. Su número de teléfono es 597-4680. José tiene 5 niños. El tiene 3 muchachos y 2 muchachas.

Story

Home

Maria lives in Los Angeles. Her address is 454 La Cienaga. Her telephone number is 957-8251. Maria has 6 children. She has 2 boys and 4 girls.

Jose lives in Long Beach. His address is 567 Miramar. His telephone number is 597-4680. Jose has 5 children. He has 3 boys and 2 girls.

Fill in the Blank

Fill in the blanks using the vocabulary words. Use each word once.

1. ¿Cuántos _____ tiene usted?

2. Yo vivo _____ Los Angeles.

3. Yo _____ 2 muchachos y 4 muchachas.

4. ¿Cuál es su número de _____ ?

5. Mi _____ de teléfono es 567-8214.

6. Yo tengo 1 _____ y 2 muchachas.

7. ¿Cuál es su _____ ?

8. ¿ _____ es su número de teléfono?

9. Yo tengo 2 muchachos y 1 _____ .

10. _____ dirección es 454 La Ciénaga.

11. Yo tengo 2 muchachos _____ 4 muchachas.

12. Yo _____ en Los Angeles.

Jumble

Unscramble the vocabulary words.

1. reent _____		muchacho
2. im _____		muchacha
3. córidnec _____		niños
4. y _____		cuál
5. áluc _____		en
6. ne _____		dirección
7. onétefol _____		vivir
8. oinsñ _____		numero
9. rviiv _____		mi
10. ahomhucc _____		tener
11. muoren _____		teléfono
12. aahcumhc _____		y

Nouns and the Definite Article

In English there is one definite article, *the*. In Spanish there are four: *el, la, los, las*. In Spanish, nouns are masculine or feminine. Nouns that refer specifically to a man such as father, brother, etc. are masculine. Nouns that refer specifically to a woman such as mother, sister, etc. are feminine. For all other nouns it is necessary to learn the proper gender. Most nouns that end in *o* are masculine. Most nouns that end in *a* are feminine. *El* and *los* modify masculine nouns. *La* and *las* modify feminine nouns.

Masculine		Feminine	
Singular	Plural	Singular	Plural
el	los	la	las

Write the following phrases in Spanish.

1. the boy

   el muchacho

2. the telephone

   _____

3. the number

   _____

4. the address

   _____

5. the girl

   _____

6. the name

   _____

7. the children

   _____

8. the United States

   _____

Fill in the blanks with el, la, los, or las.

9. ___*el*___ hermano

10. _____ mamá

11. _____ familia

12. _____ casa

13. _____ papá

14. _____ hermanas

15. _____ amigo

16. _____ hermanos

Numbers and Plurals

uno - one	seis - six
dos - two	siete - seven
tres - three	ocho - eight
cuatro - four	nueve - nine
cinco - five	diez - ten

In Spanish if a noun ends with a vowel add *s* to form the plural. If a noun ends with a consonant add *es*.

Write the following phrases in Spanish.

1. five telephones

   cinco teléfonos

2. three boys

   _____

3. seven addresses

   _____

4. ten names

   _____

5. eight children

   _____

6. two girls

   _____

7. four numbers

   _____

8. nine houses

   _____

9. six families

   _____

10. three brothers

    _____

Write the following sentences in Spanish.

11. I have six children.

    _____

12. Maria has two boys.

    _____

13. Jose has five sisters.

    _____

Answer Key

Fill in the Blank (page 12)
1. niños
2. en
3. tengo
4. teléfono
5. número
6. muchacho
7. dirección
8. Cuál
9. muchacha
10. Mi
11. y
12. vivo

Jumble (page 13)
1. tener
2. mi
3. dirección
4. y
5. cuál
6. en
7. teléfono
8. niños
9. vivir
10. muchacho
11. numero
12. muchacha

Nouns and the Definite Article (page 14)
1. el muchacho
2. el teléfono
3. el número
4. la dirección
5. la muchacha
6. el nombre
7. los niños
8. los Estados Unidos
9. el
10. la
11. la
12. la
13. el
14. las
15. el
16. los

Numbers and Plurals (page 15)
1. cinco teléfonos
2. tres muchachos
3. siete direcciones
4. diez nombres
5. ocho niños
6. dos muchachas
7. cuatro números
8. nueve casas
9. seis familias
10. tres hermanos

11. Yo tengo seis niños.
12. María tiene dos muchachos.
13. José tiene cinco hermanas.

Lección 3 Familia
Lesson 3 Family

Lista de Vocabulario	Vocabulary List
1. la mamá	1. mom
2. el papá	2. dad
3. el bebé	3. baby
4. la hermana	4. sister
5. el hermano	5. brother
6. mayor	6. older
7. menor	7. younger
8. estar	8. to be
9. la familia	9. family
10. jugar	10. to play
11. con	11. with
12. bien	12. fine

Conversación

1. Hola, Mamá.

2. ¿Dónde está mi hermano mayor?

3. Tu hermano mayor está con tu papá.

4. ¿Dónde está mi hermana menor?

5. Tu hermana menor está aquí.

6. ¿Cómo está el bebé?

7. El bebé está bien.

8. ¿Te gusta jugar con el bebé?

9. Si, me gusta jugar con el bebé.

Conversation

1. Hello, Mom.

2. Where is my older brother?

3. Your older brother is with your dad.

4. Where is my younger sister?

5. Your younger sister is here.

6. How is the baby?

7. The baby is fine.

8. Do you like to play with the baby?

9. Yes, I like to play with the baby.

Historia

Familia

María tiene un hermano y una hermana. Ella tiene un hermano mayor y una hermana menor. Su hermano vive en México y su hermana vive en Los Angeles. María tiene madre y padre. Su mamá y papá viven en Los Angeles.

José tiene dos hermanas y un hermano. El tiene dos hermanas mayores y un hermano menor. Sus dos hermanas viven en Los Angeles y su hermano menor vive en Long Beach. José tiene madre y padre. Su mamá y papá viven en Long Beach.

Story

Family

Maria has one brother and one sister. She has an older brother and a younger sister. Her brother lives in Mexico and her sister lives in Los Angeles. Maria has a mother and a father. Her mom and dad live in Los Angeles.

Jose has two sisters and one brother. He has two older sisters and one younger brother. His two sisters live in Los Angeles and his younger brother lives in Long Beach. Jose has a mother and a father. His mom and dad live in Long Beach.

Fill in the Blank

Fill in the blanks using the vocabulary words. Use each word once.

1. ¿Dónde está mi hermano _____ ?

2. Hola, _____ . ¿Dónde está mi hermana menor?

3. ¿Te gusta _____ con el bebé?

4. ¿Cómo está el _____ ?

5. El bebé está _____ .

6. Mi hermano mayor está con mi _____ .

7. Mi _____ menor está con mi mamá.

8. Mi _____ mayor está con mi papá.

9. Me gusta jugar _____ el bebé.

10. ¿Dónde está mi hermana _____ ?

11. Mi hermana menor _____ aquí.

12. Mi _____ está bien.

Jumble

Unscramble the vocabulary words.

1. alfiiam _____
2. ayrom _____
3. nibe _____
4. trase _____
5. nremhoa _____
6. aápp _____
7. ébeb _____
8. reanmah _____
9. mmaá _____
10. nemor _____
11. gruja _____
12. nco _____

mamá
papá
hermana
bebé
hermano
mayor
menor
estar
familia
jugar
con
bien

Verb Practice

tener - to have

In Spanish, it is the ending of the verb that indicates the doer of the action.

Spanish		English	
Pronoun	Verb	Pronoun	Verb
yo	tengo	I	have
*tú	tienes	you	have
él, ella, usted	tiene	he, she; you	has; have
nosotros	tenemos	we	have
**ellos, ellas, ustedes	tienen	they, you (plural)	have

*Tú is used when talking with friends, relatives, or a close associate. Usted is used when addressing someone older or someone whom you do not know well.

**Ellos is used when referring to a group of males or a group of males and females. Ellas is used when referring to a group of females.

Write the following sentences in Spanish.

1. **She has six brothers.**

   Ella tiene seis hermanos.

2. **I have five sisters.**

   _____

3. **My brother has four boys and two girls.**

   _____

4. **They (husband and wife) have three children.**

   _____

5. **We have two babies.**

   _____

6. **My family has three telephones.**

   _____

7. **You (familiar) have eight numbers.**

   _____

22

Accent Marks

In Spanish some words need accent marks. It is common practice to omit accent marks on capital letters.

All interrogative words carry a written accent.

Rewrite the following sentences putting in the correct accent marks.

1. ¿Donde esta mi hermana?

   ¿Dónde está mi hermana?

2. El bebe esta con mi mama.

   _____

3. Tu mama y papa viven en Los Angeles.

   _____

4. ¿Como esta mi hermano?

   _____

5. ¿Cual es su numero de telefono?

   _____

6. ¿Cuantos niños tiene Jose?

   _____

7. ¿Te gusta jugar con mi hermano?

   _____

8. ¿Donde vive Maria?

   _____

Answer Key

Fill in the Blank (page 20)

1. mayor or menor
2. mamá
3. jugar
4. bebé
5. bien
6. papá
7. hermana
8. hermano
9. con
10. menor or mayor
11. está
12. familia

Jumble (page 21)

1. familia
2. mayor
3. bien
4. estar
5. hermano
6. papá
7. bebé
8. hermana
9. mamá
10. menor
11. jugar
12. con

Verb Practice (page 22)

1. Ella tiene seis hermanos.
2. Yo tengo cinco hermanas.
3. Mi hermano tiene cuatro muchachos y dos muchachas.
4. Ellos tienen tres niños.
5. Nosotros tenemos dos bebés.
6. Mi familia tiene tres teléfonos.
7. Tú tienes ocho números.

Accent Marks (page 23)

1. ¿Dónde está mi hermana?
2. El bebé está con mi mamá.
3. Tu mamá y papá viven en Los Angeles.
4. ¿Cómo está mi hermano?
5. ¿Cuál es su número de teléfono?
6. ¿Cuántos niños tiene José?
7. ¿Te gusta jugar con mi hermano?
8. ¿Dónde vive María?

Lección 4 La Hora
Lesson 4 Telling Time

Lista de Vocabulario	Vocabulary List
1. cinco	1. five
2. tu	2. your *(familiar)*
3. la hora	3. time; hour
4. el trabajo	4. work
5. empezar	5. to start
6. reloj	6. clock; watch
7. aquí	7. here
8. la casa	8. house; home
9. ir	9. to go
10. cenar	10. to have supper
11. ocho	11. eight
12. ¿qué?	12. what?

Conversación

1. ¿Qué hora es?
2. Son las cinco.
3. ¿A qué hora empieza tu trabajo?
4. Empieza a las ocho.
5. ¿A qué hora te vas a la casa?
6. Me voy a la casa a las cinco.
7. ¿A qué hora cenas tú?
8. Yo ceno a las seis.
9. ¿A qué hora te acuestas?
10. Me acuesto a las diez.
11. ¿A qué hora te levantas por la mañana?
12. Me levanto a las seis.

Conversation

1. What time is it?
2. It is five o'clock.
3. At what time does your work start?
4. It starts at eight o'clock.
5. At what time do you go home?
6. I go home at 5 o'clock.
7. At what time do you have dinner?
8. I have dinner at 6 o'clock.
9. At what time do you go to bed?
10. I go to bed at 10 o'clock.
11. At what time do you get up in the morning?
12. I get up at 6 o'clock.

Historia

El Reloj

María se levanta a las seis. Su trabajo empieza a las ocho. A María le gusta su trabajo. Ella regresa a la casa a las cinco. María cena a las seis. A ella le gusta jugar con sus niños. María se acuesta a las diez.

José se levanta a las cinco. Su trabajo empieza a las siete. A José le gusta su trabajo. El regresa a su casa a las cuatro. José cena a las seis. A él le gusta jugar con sus niños. José se acuesta a las nueve.

Story

The Clock

Maria gets up at six o'clock. Her work starts at eight o'clock. Maria likes her work. She goes home at five o'clock. Maria has dinner at six o'clock. She likes to play with her children. At ten o'clock Maria goes to bed.

Jose gets up at five o'clock. His work starts at seven o'clock. Jose likes his work. He goes home at four o'clock. Jose has dinner at six o'clock. He likes to play with his children. At nine o'clock Jose goes to bed.

Fill in the Blank

Fill in the blanks using the vocabulary words. Use each word once.

1. Son las _____ .

2. ¿A qué hora _____ tú?

3. Me levanto a las _____ .

4. ¿Qué _____ es?

5. ¿A _____ hora te acuestas?

6. ¿A qué hora te vas a la _____ ?

7. ¿A qué hora empieza _____ trabajo?

8. Mi _____ empieza a las nueve.

9. Mi _____ está en la mesa.

10. _____ tiene la cena.

11. Mi trabajo _____ a las ocho.

12. Me _____ para la casa a las cinco.

Matching

Match up the Spanish and English words.

1. _____ to start

2. _____ eight

3. _____ to have dinner

4. _____ here

5. _____ work

6. _____ to go

7. _____ time

8. _____ clock

9. _____ your

10. _____ five

11. _____ what?

12. _____ house

cinco
tu
hora
empezar
reloj
aquí
casa
ir
trabajo
cenar
ocho
¿qué?

29

Verb Practice

estar - to be

In Spanish, it is the ending of the verb that indicates the doer of the action.

Spanish		English	
Pronoun	Verb	Pronoun	Verb
yo	estoy	I	am
*tú	estás	you	are
el, ella, usted	está	he, she; you	is; are
nosotros	estamos	we	are
**ellos, ellas, ustedes	están	they, you (plural)	are

*Tú is used when talking with friends, relatives, or a close associate. Usted is used when addressing someone older or someone whom you do not know well.

**Ellos is used when referring to a group of males or a group of males and females. Ellas is used when referring to a group of females.

Write the following sentences in Spanish.

1. How are you? *(formal)*

   _____

2. I am fine. Thank you.

   _____

3. The girls are in the house.

   _____

4. We are in Los Angeles.

   _____

5. What time is it?

   _____

6. Maria is fine.

   _____

7. You *(familiar)* are in the United States.

   _____

30

Possessive Adjectives

Possessive adjectives are used to show ownership or possession.

The possessive adjectives in Spanish are:

mi - my

tu - your *(familiar)*

su - his, her, your *(formal)*, their

nuestro, nuestra - our

An *s* is added to the possessive adjective when modifying more than one person or thing. For example: <u>mis</u> *hermanos;* <u>tus</u> *teléfonos*.

Nuestro is used with masculine nouns. *Nuestra* is used with feminine nouns. For example: *nuestra casa; nuestro bebé.*

Although *su* can mean his, her, their or your (formal), the exact meaning is usually clear from the context of the sentence.

Write the following sentences in Spanish.

1. **Where is my sister?**

   _____

2. **Your** *(familiar)* **sister is in the house.**

   _____

3. **Where is our papa?**

   _____

4. **His brother is in Los Angeles.**

   _____

5. **Our address is 564 La Cienaga.**

   _____

6. **Her brothers are here.**

   _____

7. **Their children are in Mexico.**

   _____

Answer Key

Fill in the Blank (page 28)

1. cinco o ocho
2. cenas
3. ocho o cinco
4. hora
5. qué
6. casa
7. tu
8. trabajo
9. reloj
10. Aquí
11. empieza
12. voy

Matching (page 29)

1. empezar
2. ocho
3. cenar
4. aquí
5. trabajo
6. ir
7. hora
8. reloj
9. tu
10. cinco
11. ¿qué?
12. casa

Verb Practice (page 30)

1. ¿Cómo está usted?
2. Estoy bien. Gracias.
3. Las muchachas están en la casa.
4. Nosotros estamos en Los Angeles.
5. ¿Qué hora es?
6. María está bien.
7. Tú estás en los Estados Unidos.

Possessive Adjectives (page 31)

1. ¿Dónde está mi hermana?
2. Tu hermana está en la casa.
3. ¿Dónde está nuestro papá?
4. Su hermano está en Los Angeles.
5. Nuestra dirección es 564 La Ciénaga.
6. Sus hermanos están aquí.
7. Sus niños están en México.

Lección 5 Números
Lesson 5 Numbers

Lista de Vocabulario	Vocabulary List
1. tres	1. three
2. el amigo la amiga	2. friend
3. dos	3. two
4. o	4. or
5. las personas	5. people
6. su	6. your *(formal)*, his, her, their
7. él	7. he
8. cuatro	8. four
9. ella	9. she
10. siete	10. seven
11. bonito; bonita	11. pretty
12. ser	12. to be

Conversación

1. ¿Cuántas personas son en tu familia?

2. Hay siete personas en mi familia.

3. ¿Cuántos son muchachos?

4. Hay dos muchachos.

5. ¿Cuántas son muchachas?

6. Hay tres muchachas.

7. ¿Cuántas hermanas tienes tú?

8. Tengo tres hermanas.

9. ¿Cuántos hermanos tienes tú?

10. Tengo un hermano.

Conversation

1. How many people are in your family?

2. There are seven people in my family.

3. How many are boys?

4. There are two boys.

5. How many are girls?

6. There are three girls.

7. How many sisters do you have?

8. I have three sisters.

9. How many brothers do you have?

10. I have one brother.

Historia

Amigos

María tiene muchas amigas. Ella tiene siete amigas que viven en Los Angeles. María tiene cuatro amigas que viven en Long Beach. Tres de sus amigas son muy bonitas. Sus niños tienen muchos amigos. Dos de sus amigos viven cerca.

José tiene muchos amigos. El tiene siete amigos en su trabajo. José va al trabajo con tres amigos. Cuatro de sus amigos empiezan a trabajar a las ocho. Después del trabajo José va a su casa con dos amigos.

Story

Friends

Maria has many friends. She has seven friends who live in Los Angeles. Maria has four friends who live in Long Beach. Three of her friends are very pretty. Her children have many friends. Two of their friends live nearby.

Jose has many friends. He has seven friends at his work. Jose goes to work with three friends. Four of his friends start work at eight o'clock. After work Jose goes home with two friends.

Fill in the Blank

Fill in the blanks using the vocabulary words. Use each word once.

1. María tiene muchas _____ .

2. ¿Cuántas _____ son en tu familia?

3. María tiene _____ amigas que viven en Los Angeles.

4. José tiene muchos amigos. A _____ le gustan su amigos.

5. Ella es muy _____ .

6. María tiene _____ amigas que viven en Long Beach.

7. _____ de sus amigas son muy bonitas.

8. María vive en Los Angeles. _____ tiene muchas amigas.

9. _____ de sus amigos viven cerca.

10. ¿Cuántas personas son en _____ familia?

11. ¿Vives en Long Beach _____ en Los Angeles?

12. Tres de sus amigas _____ muy bonitas.

Alphabetical Order

Below is the Spanish alphabet. It has 30 letters. The underlined letters are not in the English alphabet.

a b c <u>ch</u> d e f g h i j k l <u>ll</u> m n <u>ñ</u> o p q r <u>rr</u> s t u v w x y z.

Write the vocabulary words (at the right) in alphabetical order.

1. _____

2. _____

3. _____

4. _____

5. _____

6. _____

7. _____

8. _____

9. _____

10. _____

11. _____

12. _____

tres
amigo
dos
o
personas
su
él
cuatro
ella
siete
bonita
ser

Verb Practice

ser - to be

In Spanish there are two verbs for *to be*: *ser* and *estar*. *Ser* is used to express *Who is?* or *What is?* *Estar* is used to express *place, where, or health*.

Spanish		English	
Pronoun	Verb	Pronoun	Verb
yo	soy	I	am
tú *(familiar)*	eres	you	are
él, ella, usted	es	he, she; you	is; are
nosotros	somos	we	are
ellos, ellas, ustedes	son	they; you (plural)	are

Write the following sentences in Spanish.

1. **What time is it?**

    _____

2. **The boys are in the house.**

    _____

3. **The girl is very pretty.**

    _____

4. **How is your *(familiar)* father?**

    _____

5. **Where is your *(familiar)* house?**

    _____

6. **How many people are in your *(formal)* family?**

    _____

7. **I am from Mexico.**

    _____

8. **You *(familiar)* are very pretty.**

    _____

¿Cuál? vs. ¿Qué?

¿Cuál? and ¿Qué? both mean *What?*.

In Spanish the most common interrogative word used with the verb ser is ¿Cuál?.

¿Cuál? is used when asking for a selection within a group.

¿Qué? is used when asking for a definition.

¿Cuál? also corresponds to the English *Which?*. ¿Cuáles? means *Which ones?*.

Fill in the blanks with ¿Cuál?, ¿Cuáles? or ¿Qué?.

1. ¿ _____ es tu número de teléfono?

2. ¿ _____ es tu casa?

3. ¿ _____ hora es?

4. ¿ _____ son tus hermanas?

5. ¿ _____ es su dirección?

6. ¿A _____ hora empieza tu trabajo?

7. ¿ _____ son tus amigos?

8. ¿A _____ hora te levantas por la mañana?

9. ¿A _____ hora tienes la cena?

10. ¿ _____ tiene el bebé?

Answer Key

Fill in the Blank (page 36)

1.	amigas	7.	Tres
2.	personas	8.	Ella
3.	siete	9.	Dos
4.	él	10.	su
5.	bonita	11.	o
6.	cuatro	12.	son

Alphabetical Order (page 37)

1.	amigo	7.	o
2.	bonita	8.	personas
3.	cuatro	9.	ser
4.	dos	10.	siete
5.	él	11.	su
6.	ella	12.	tres

Verb Practice (page 38)
1. ¿Qué hora es?
2. Los muchachos están en la casa.
3. La muchacha es muy bonita.
4. ¿Cómo está tu papá?
5. ¿Dónde está tu casa?
6. ¿Cuántas personas son en su familia?
7. Soy de México.
8. Tú eres muy bonita.

¿Cuál? vs. ¿Qué? (page 39)

1.	Cuál	6.	qué
2.	Cuál	7.	Cuáles
3.	Qué	8.	qué
4.	Cuáles	9.	qué
5.	Cuál	10.	Qué

Lección 6 Colores
Lesson 6 Colors

Lista de Vocabulario	Vocabulary List
1. el carro	1. car
2. el ojo	2. eye
3. azul	3. blue
4. nuevo; nueva	4. new
5. dar	5. to give
6. rojo; roja	6. red
7. café	7. brown
8. el pelo	8. hair
9. ¿cuándo?	9. when?
10. el vestido	10. dress
11. los zapatos	11. shoes
12. verde	12. green

Conversación

1. ¿Tienes un vestido nuevo?

2. Si, mi madre me lo dio.

3. Me gusta tu vestido azul.

4. Gracias.

5. Me gustan sus zapatos cafés.

6. Gracias. ¿De qué color son tus ojos?

7. Mis ojos son verdes.

8. ¿De qué color es tu casa?

9. Mi casa es roja.

10. ¿De qué color es tu carro?

11. Mi carro es azul.

Conversation

1. Do you have a new dress?

2. Yes, my mother gave it to me.

3. I like your blue dress.

4. Thank you.

5. I like your brown shoes.

6. Thank you. What color are your eyes?

7. My eyes are green.

8. What color is your house?

9. My house is red.

10. What color is your car?

11. My car is blue.

Historia

María y José

La casa de María es roja. María tiene un carro nuevo. Su carro es azul. A ella le gusta su carro nuevo. María tiene los ojos cafés. Sus ojos son bonitos. El pelo de María es café. El vestido de María es verde. El vestido es nuevo. Los zapatos de María son verdes.

La casa de José es verde. José tiene un carro nuevo. Su carro es rojo. A él le gusta su carro rojo. José tiene los ojos cafés. Sus ojos son grandes. El pelo de José es café. La camisa de José es azul. La camisa es nueva. Los zapatos de José son cafés.

Story

Maria and Jose

Maria's house is red. Maria has a new car. Her car is blue. She likes her new car. Maria has brown eyes. Her eyes are pretty. Maria's hair is brown. Maria's dress is green. The dress is new. Maria's shoes are green.

Jose's house is green. Jose has a new car. His car is red. He likes his new car. Jose has brown eyes. His eyes are big. Jose's hair is brown. Jose's shirt is blue. The shirt is new. Jose's shoes are brown.

Fill in the Blank

Fill in the blanks using the vocabulary words. Use each word once.

1. La casa de María es _____ .

2. Los _____ de José son cafés.

3. El vestido de María es _____ .

4. El _____ de José es rojo.

5. Los ojos de José son _____ .

6. El _____ de María es café.

7. La camisa de José es _____ .

8. Los _____ de María son verdes.

9. Su _____ es verde.

10. La casa de José es _____ .

11. ¿ _____ empieza tu trabajo?

Jumble

Unscramble the vocabulary words.

1. lauz _____
2. féca _____
3. siotevd _____
4. loep _____
5. ooj _____
6. redev _____
7. toaszpa _____
8. eonuv _____
9. rad _____
10. dunocá _____
11. racor _____
12. jroo _____

carro
ojo
azul
nuevo
dar
rojo
café
pelo
cuándo
vestido
zapatos
verde

Adjectives - Colors

amarillo - yellow
anaranjado - orange
azul - blue
café - brown
morado - purple
negro - black
rojo - red
verde - green
blanco – white

In Spanish descriptive adjectives follow the noun. Each adjective must agree with the noun it modifies. Adjectives that end in *o* have four forms:

el vestido rojo - the red dress
los vestidos rojos - the red dresses
la casa roja - the red house
las casas rojas - the red houses

Adjectives that end in *e* have two forms, singular and plural:

la camisa verde - the green shirt
las camisas verdes - the green shirts

Most adjectives that end in a consonant have only two forms, singular and plural:

la camisa azul
los ojos azules

Write the following phrases in Spanish.

1. the red telephone
   el teléfono rojo

2. my green dress
   _____

3. the black cars
   _____

4. our pretty baby
   _____

5. my purple shoes
   _____

6. their new cars
   _____

7. the pretty girls
   _____

8. your *(familiar)* blue shoes
   _____

9. his pretty sister
   _____

10. the white shirt
    _____

11. the orange dresses
    _____

12. the yellow house
    _____

Verb Practice

vivir - to live

In Spanish, it is the ending of the verb that indicates the doer of the action.

Spanish		English	
Pronoun	Verb	Pronoun	Verb
yo	vivo	I	live
tú (familiar)	vives	you	live
él, ella, usted	vive	he, she; you	lives; live
nosotros	vivimos	we	live
ellos, ellas, ustedes	viven	they, you (plural)	live

Write the following sentences in Spanish.

1. They live in Los Angeles.

_____

2. Jose lives in Long Beach.

_____

3. Where do you *(familiar)* live?

_____

4. I live in San Diego.

_____

5. We live in the United States.

_____

6. She lives in the house.

_____

7. The girls live in Mexico.

_____

8. Where do they live?

_____

Answer Key

Fill in the Blank (page 44)

1. roja
2. ojos
3. nuevo
4. carro
5. cafés
6. pelo
7. azul
8. zapatos
9. vestido
10. verde
11. Cuándo

Jumble (page 45)

1. azul
2. café
3. vestido
4. pelo
5. ojo
6. verde
7. zapatos
8. nuevo
9. dar
10. cuándo
11. carro
12. rojo

Adjectives - Colors (page 46)

1. el teléfono rojo
2. mi vestido verde
3. los carros negros
4. nuestro bebé bonito
5. mis zapatos morados
6. sus carros nuevos
7. las muchachas bonitas
8. tus zapatos azules
9. su hermana bonita
10. la camisa blanca
11. los vestidos anaranjados
12. la casa amarilla

Verb Practice (page 47)

1. Ellos viven en Los Angeles.
2. José vive en Long Beach.
3. ¿Dónde vives tú?
4. Yo vivo en San Diego.
5. Nosotros vivimos en los Estados Unidos.
6. Ella vive en la casa.
7. Las muchachas viven en México.
8. ¿Dónde viven ellos?

Lección 7 Partes del Cuerpo
Lesson 7 Parts of the Body

Lista de Vocabulario	Vocabulary List
1. la nariz	1. nose
2. los oídos	2. ears
3. querer	3. to want
4. el plátano	4. banana
5. la cabeza	5. head
6. amarillo	6. yellow
7. la mano	7. hand
8. me	8. me
9. el beso	9. kiss
10. la boca	10. mouth
11. amar	11. to love
12. ¿cuántos?	12. how many?

Conversación

1. Hola, bebé. ¿Cómo estás?

2. ¿Dónde está tu nariz?

3. Aquí está tu nariz.

4. ¿Dónde están tus oídos?

5. Ellos están en tu cabeza.

6. Dame tu mano.

7. Aquí está mi mano.

8. ¡Quítatelo de la boca!

9. ¿Quieres un plátano?

10. Ponlo en tu boca.

11. Dame un beso.

12. Gracias, yo te amo.

Conversation

1. Hi, baby. How are you?

2. Where is your nose?

3. Here is your nose.

4. Where are your ears?

5. They are on your head.

6. Give me your hand.

7. Here is my hand.

8. Take that out of your mouth!

9. Do you want a banana?

10. Put it in your mouth.

11. Give me a kiss.

12. Thanks, I love you.

Historia

Jugando con los Niños

María juega con su bebé. María le da un plátano al bebé. El bebé pone el plátano en su boca. María le da un beso al bebé. El bebé le da un beso a María. María pone su mano en el bebé. María ama a su bebé.

José está en la casa con sus niños. Su muchacha pequeña quiere un plátano. José le da un plátano a la muchacha. Su muchacho pequeño juega con un carro rojo. Al muchacho pequeño le gusta el carro. José tiene un bebé. José le da un beso a su bebé. José ama a sus niños.

Story

Playing with the Children

Maria plays with her baby. She gives the baby a banana. The baby puts the banana in her mouth. Maria gives the baby a kiss. The baby gives Maria a kiss. Maria puts her hand on the baby. Maria loves her baby.

Jose is at home with his children. His little girl wants a banana. Jose gives a banana to the girl. His little boy plays with a red car. The little boy likes the car. Jose has a baby. Jose gives his baby a kiss. Jose loves his children.

Fill in the Blank

Fill in the blanks using the vocabulary words. Use each word once.

1. Aquí está mi _____ .

2. Me gusta tu vestido _____ .

3. Yo te _____ .

4. ¿ _____ hermanos tienes tú?

5. ¿Dónde está tu _____ ?

6. El bebé pone el plátano en su _____ .

7. La muchacha _____ un plátano.

8. Dame un _____ .

9. Tus _____ están en tu cabeza.

10. El bebé quiere un _____ .

11. Da_____ tu mano.

12. El bebé tiene dos oídos en su _____ .

Jumble

Unscramble the vocabulary words.

1. _____ em		nariz
2. _____ ídoso		oídos
3. _____ sutácon		querer
4. _____ namo		plátano
5. _____ razin		cabeza
6. _____ zecbaa		amarillo
7. _____ rueqre		mano
8. _____ coba		me
9. _____ larmolia		beso
10. _____ sboe		boca
11. _____ raam		amar
12. _____ napoált		cuántos

Verb Practice

gustar - to like

Gustar is a special kind of verb which is used with a set of pronouns called indirect object pronouns. Gustar is normally used in the 3rd person singular or plural, depending on the number of the noun which follows. The verb must be preceded by an indirect object pronoun.

Spanish		English	
Indirect Object Pronoun	Verb	Pronoun	Verb
me	gusta/gustan	I	like
te	gusta/gustan	you	like
le	gusta/gustan	he, she; you *(formal)*	likes; like
nos	gusta/gustan	we	like
les	gusta/gustan	they, you *(plural)*	like

Example: Me <u>gusta</u> tu <u>vestido</u>.
Me <u>gustan</u> los <u>zapatos</u>.

Write the following sentences in Spanish.

1. I like your *(familiar)* house.

   _____

2. Do you *(familiar)* like the United States?

   _____

3. They like the new car.

   _____

4. She likes the green shoes.

   _____

5. We like the red dresses.

   _____

6. I like your *(familiar)* children.

   _____

7. He likes the yellow shirt.

   _____

The Indefinite Article

The indefinite articles (a, an) are *un* and *una* in Spanish. *Un* is used with masculine nouns and *una* is used with feminine nouns.

un carro
una muchacha

Rewrite the following sentences replacing the definite article with an indefinite article.

1. José tiene el carro nuevo.

   _____

2. Mi familia vive en la casa roja.

   _____

3. Mi hermana tiene el vestido amarillo.

   _____

4. Ellos viven en la casa grande.

   _____

5. Tu amiga tiene el teléfono azul.

   _____

6. Ella me dio la camisa blanca.

   _____

7. Aquí tiene el plátano.

   _____

8. Ellos me dieron el reloj nuevo.

   _____

Answer Key

Fill in the Blank (page 52)

1.	mano	7.	quiere
2.	amarillo	8.	beso
3.	amo	9.	oídos
4.	Cuántos	10.	plátano
5.	nariz	11.	me
6.	boca	12.	cabeza

Jumble (page 53)

1.	me	7.	querer
2.	oídos	8.	boca
3.	cuántos	9.	amarillo
4.	mano	10.	beso
5.	nariz	11.	amar
6.	cabeza	12.	plátano

Verb Practice (page 54)

1. Me gusta tu casa.
2. ¿Te gustan los Estados Unidos?
3. Les gusta el carro nuevo.
4. Le gustan los zapatos verdes.
5. Nos gustan los vestidos rojos.
6. Me gustan tus niños.
7. Le gusta la camisa amarilla.

Indefinite Article (page 55)

1. José tiene un carro nuevo.
2. Mi familia vive en una casa roja.
3. Mi hermana tiene un vestido amarillo.
4. Ellos viven en una casa grande.
5. Tu amiga tiene un teléfono azul.
6. Ella me dio una camisa blanca.
7. Aquí tiene un plátano.
8. Ellos me dieron un reloj nuevo.

Lección 8 Desayuno
Lesson 8 Breakfast

Lista de Vocabulario

1. la leche
2. el huevo
3. también
4. el desayuno
5. la taza
6. comer
7. el azúcar
8. la mañana
9. el pan
10. el café
11. el tocino
12. tomar

Vocabulary List

1. milk
2. egg
3. also
4. breakfast
5. cup
6. to eat
7. sugar
8. morning
9. bread
10. coffee
11. bacon
12. to take; to drink

Conversación

1. ¿A qué hora comes el desayuno?

2. Como a las siete por la mañana.

3. ¿Qué comiste esta mañana?

4. Comí dos huevos, tocino, y jugo de naranja.

5. ¿Comiste algo más?

6. Sí, también comí pan tostado con jalea y leche.

7. ¿Te gustaría una taza de café?

8. Sí, me gustaría una taza de café.

9. ¿Quieres crema y azúcar?

10. Gracias. Lo tomo con leche.

11. ¿Qué haces después del desayuno?

12. Me voy al trabajo.

Conversation

1. What time do you eat breakfast?

2. I eat at seven o'clock in the morning.

3. What did you eat this morning?

4. I had two eggs, bacon, and orange juice.

5. Did you have anything else?

6. Yes, I also had toast with jelly and milk.

7. Would you like a cup of coffee?

8. Yes, I would like a cup of coffee.

9. Do you want cream and sugar?

10. Thank you. I drink it with milk.

11. What do you do after breakfast?

12. I go to work.

Historia

Desayuno

María come el desayuno a las ocho. Ella come huevos y tocino. A María le gusta el desayuno. Después del desayuno va a trabajar. En el trabajo toma una taza de café. A María le gustan leche y azúcar con su café. Cuando María regresa a su casa come un plátano.

José toma el desayuno a las seis. El come pan tostado con jalea, jugo de naranja, y café. Toma su café con leche. Después del desayuno José va a trabajar. En el trabajo él toma leche. Cuando José regresa a la casa come un plátano también.

Story

Breakfast

Maria eats breakfast at eight o'clock. She eats eggs and bacon. Maria likes breakfast. After breakfast she goes to work. At work she drinks a cup of coffee. Maria likes milk and sugar with her coffee. When Maria goes home she eats a banana.

Jose eats breakfast at six o'clock. He has toast with jelly, orange juice, and coffee. He drinks his coffee with milk. After breakfast Jose goes to work. At work he drinks milk. When Jose goes home he eats a banana also.

Fill in the Blank

Fill in the blanks using the vocabulary words. Use each word once.

1. María toma una taza de _____ .

2. Ella come _____ y huevos.

3. Después del _____ , María va al trabajo.

4. A María le gusta su café con leche y _____ .

5. José come el desayuno a las seis por

   la _____ .

6. María toma una _____ de café con

   leche y azúcar.

7. Ella come dos _____ en el desayuno.

8. José come _____ con jalea.

9. María _____ su café con leche y azúcar.

10. María _____ huevos y tocino en el desayuno.

11. María _____ come pan.

12. María toma su café con _____ y azúcar.

Matching

Match up the Spanish and English words.

1. _____ sugar

2. _____ egg

3. _____ bread

4. _____ breakfast

5. _____ bacon

6. _____ cup

7. _____ also

8. _____ to eat

9. _____ to drink

10. _____ milk

11. _____ coffee

12. _____ morning

leche
huevo
también
desayuno
taza
comer
azúcar
mañana
pan
café
tocino
tomar

Showing Possession

One frequent way of expressing possession in Spanish is by using the preposition *de* with a noun or pronoun to show possession.

El vestido de María es azul. - Maria's dress is blue.

Write the following sentences in Spanish.

1. I like Jose's shoes.

   _____

2. Maria's house is red.

   _____

3. My sister's eyes are green.

   _____

4. Maria's watch is new.

   _____

5. Do you like Jose's new shirt?

   _____

6. My brother's hair is brown.

   _____

7. Maria's friend is very pretty.

   _____

8. Jose's address is 567 Miramar.

   _____

Direct Object Pronouns

The direct object pronouns in Spanish are *lo, los, la, las*. *Lo* and *los* are masculine pronouns. *La* and *las* are feminine pronouns. They refer to either persons or things and precede the conjugated form of the verb.

José come el pan. - Jose eats the bread.
José lo come. - Jose eats it.

Rewrite the following sentences substituting the underlined object with a direct object pronoun.

1. Yo tengo <u>las camisas amarillas</u>.

   _____

2. Yo amo <u>a mi bebé</u>.

   _____

3. Ellos toman <u>la leche</u> en el desayuno.

   _____

4. Mi hermana quiere <u>los zapatos</u>.

   _____

5. Aquí tiene <u>el teléfono</u>.

   _____

6. Yo di <u>un reloj</u> a mi hermano.

   _____

7. Yo como <u>los huevos</u> en el desayuno.

   _____

8. El bebé come <u>el plátano</u>.

   _____

Answer Key

Fill in the Blank (page 60)

1.	café	7.	huevos
2.	tocino	8.	pan
3.	desayuno	9.	toma
4.	azúcar	10.	come
5.	mañana	11.	también
6.	taza	12.	leche

Matching (page 61)

1.	azúcar	7.	también
2.	huevo	8.	comer
3.	pan	9.	tomar
4.	desayuno	10.	leche
5.	tocino	11.	café
6.	taza	12.	mañana

Showing Possession (page 62)
1. Me gustan los zapatos de José.
2. La casa de María es roja.
3. Los ojos de mi hermana son verdes.
4. El reloj de María es nuevo.
5. ¿Te gusta la camisa nueva de José?
6. El pelo de mi hermano es café.
7. La amiga de María es muy bonita.
8. La dirección de José es 567 Miramar.

Direct Object Pronouns (page 63)
1. Yo las tengo.
2. Yo lo amo.
3. Ellos la toman en el desayuno.
4. Mi hermana los quiere.
5. Aquí lo tiene.
6. Yo lo di a mi hermano.
7. Yo los como en el desayuno.
8. El bebé lo come.

Lección 9 Una Visita al Doctor
Lesson 9 A Visit to the Doctor

Lista de Vocabulario

1. enfermo(a)
2. la fiebre
3. dormir
4. más
5. la cita
6. el helado
7. el almuerzo
8. la cena
9. el hijo
10. la hija
11. la influenza
12. la medicina
13. el catarro
14. llevar
15. después

Vocabulary List

1. sick
2. fever
3. to sleep
4. more
5. appointment
6. ice cream
7. lunch
8. dinner
9. son
10. daughter
11. flu
12. medicine
13. cold
14. to take
15. after

Conversación

1. Llevo a mi hijo al doctor.

2. ¿Qué es lo que tiene?

3. El tiene fiebre y náuseas.

4. ¿A qué hora es la cita?

5. A las diez de la mañana.

6. Hola, Doctor. Mi hijo está enfermo.

7. ¿Cuántos años tiene?

8. El tiene dos años.

9. ¿Cómo se llama su hijo?

10. Se llama Enrique.

11. Permítame examinarlo. El tiene la influenza. Le daré alguna medicina.

12. Gracias, Doctor.

Conversation

1. I am taking my son to the doctor.

2. What is the matter with him?

3. He has a fever and is sick to his stomach.

4. At what time is the appointment?

5. At ten o'clock in the morning.

6. Hello, Doctor. My son is sick.

7. How old is he?

8. He is two years old.

9. What is your son's name?

10. His name is Enrique.

11. Let me examine him. He has the flu. I will give him some medicine.

12. Thank you, Doctor.

Historia

Los Niños Están Enfermos

Carmen es la hija de José. Ella tiene ocho años. Carmen está enferma. Tiene catarro. Carmen no puede ir a la escuela. Tiene que guardar cama y tomar su medicina. Para el desayuno, José le da pan y jugo de naranja. Después del desayuno, Carmen mira la televisión. Para el almuerzo ella come sopa y helado. Después del almuerzo, Carmen duerme un poco. Más tarde Carmen lee un libro. Para la cena ella toma más sopa. Carmen se acuesta temprano. Mañana podrá ir a la escuela.

Enrique es el hijo de María. El es un bebé. Enrique está enfermo. Tiene fiebre y náuseas. María le da agua y pan. No come mucho. María lo lleva al doctor. Enrique tiene la influenza. El doctor le da medicina.

Story

The Children Are Sick

Carmen is the daughter of Jose. She is eight years old. Carmen is sick. She has a cold. Carmen can not go to school. She has to stay in bed and take her medicine. For breakfast Jose gives her bread and orange juice. After breakfast Carmen watches TV. For lunch she eats soup and ice cream. After lunch Carmen sleeps a little. Later Carmen reads a book. For dinner she has more soup. Carmen goes to bed early. Tomorrow she can go to school.

Enrique is the son of Maria. He is a baby. Enrique is sick. He has a fever and is sick to his stomach. Maria gives him water and bread. He does not eat much. Maria takes him to the doctor. Enrique has the flu. The doctor gives him medicine.

Fill in the Blank

Fill in the blanks using the vocabulary words. Use each word once.

1. María tiene una _____ con el doctor.

2. Enrique tiene una _____ alta.

3. Para la _____ Carmen toma sopa.

4. Después del almuerzo, Carmen _____ un poco.

5. Carmen no puede ir a la escuela. Ella tiene

   _____ .

6. Enrique está enfermo. El toma su _____ .

7. Enrique tiene la _____ .

8. Carmen está _____ . Tiene catarro.

9. Enrique es el _____ de María.

10. _____ del almuerzo, Carmen duerme un poco.

11. Carmen toma sopa y _____ para el almuerzo.

12. Carmen es la _____ de José.

13. María _____ a Enrique al doctor.

14. Carmen toma _____ sopa para la cena.

15. Para el _____ Carmen toma sopa y helado.

Alphabetical Order

Below is the Spanish alphabet. It has 30 letters. The underlined letters are not in the English alphabet.

a b c <u>ch</u> d e f g h i j k l <u>ll</u> m n <u>ñ</u> o p q r <u>rr</u> s t u v w x y z.

Write the vocabulary words (at the right) in alphabetical order.

1. _____

2. _____

3. _____

4. _____

5. _____

6. _____

7. _____

8. _____

9. _____

10. _____

11. _____

12. _____

13. _____

14. _____

15. _____

enfermo
fiebre
dormir
más
cita
helado
almuerzo
cena
hijo
hija
influenza
medicina
catarro
llevar
después

Indirect Object Pronouns

The indirect object pronouns are:

me - to me
te - to you *(familiar)*
le - to him, to her, to you *(formal)*
nos - to us
les - to them, to you *(plural)*

The indirect object pronoun receives the indirect action of the verb or indicates for whom or to whom something is done.

The indirect object pronoun precedes the conjugated verb.

Rewrite the following sentences substituting the underlined indirect object with a pronoun. The first one has been done for you.

1. Mamá da plátanos <u>a los niños</u>.

   Mamá les da plátanos.

2. Yo hablo <u>con mi abuela</u> todos los días.

   _____

3. Carlos escribe una carta <u>a su amigo</u>.

   _____

4. El señor García habla <u>a sus hijos</u>.

   _____

5. Papá da el desayuno <u>a nosotros</u>.

   _____

6. El habla <u>a los niños</u> en voz alta.

   _____

7. Los muchachos dan sus números de teléfono <u>a las muchachas</u>.

   _____

Verb Practice

comer - to eat

In Spanish, it is the ending of the verb that indicates the doer of the action.

Spanish		English	
Pronoun	Verb	Pronoun	Verb
yo	como	I	eat
tú	comes	you	eat
él, ella, usted	come	he, she; you	eats; eat
nosotros	comemos	we	eat
ellos, ellas, ustedes	comen	they, you *(plural)*	eat

Write the following sentences in Spanish.

1. She eats bread and cereal for breakfast.

   _____

2. They eat soup and carrots for lunch.

   _____

3. For dinner we eat meat, vegetables, and fruit.

   _____

4. I eat an apple after school.

   _____

5. You (informal) do not eat very much for breakfast.

   _____

6. He does not eat meat.

   _____

7. On Fridays, my sister and I eat dinner at my grandmother's house.

   _____

8. Our two dogs eat a lot.

   _____

Answer Key

Fill in the Blank (page 68)

1. cita
2. fiebre
3. cena
4. duerme
5. catarro
6. medicina
7. influenza
8. enferma
9. hijo
10. Después
11. helado
12. hija
13. lleva
14. más
15. almuerzo

Alphabetical Order (page 69)

1. almuerzo
2. catarro
3. cena
4. cita
5. después
6. dormir
7. enfermo
8. fiebre
9. helado
10. hija
11. hijo
12. influenza
13. llevar
14. más
15. medicina

Indirect Object Pronouns (page 70)

1. Mamá les da plátanos.
2. Yo le hablo todos los días.
3. Carlos le escribe una carta.
4. El señor García les habla.
5. Papá nos da el desayuno.
6. El les habla en voz alta.
7. Los muchachos les dan sus números de teléfono.

Verb Practice (page 71)

1. Ella come pan y cereal en el desayuno.
2. Comen sopa y zanahorias para el almuerzo.
3. Para la cena comemos carne, legumbres, y fruta.
4. Yo como una manzana después de la escuela.
5. Tú no comes mucho en el desayuno.
6. El no come carne.
7. Los viernes, mi hermana y yo comemos la cena en la casa de mi abuela.
8. Nuestros dos perros comen mucho.

Lección 10 En la Escuela
Lesson 10 At School

Lista de Vocabulario	Vocabulary List
1. buenos días	1. good morning
2. ahora	2. now
3. estudiar	3. to study
4. las matemáticas	4. mathematics (math)
5. el pizarrón	5. board
6. la multiplicación	6. multiplication
7. el recreo	7. recess
8. formar fila	8. to line up
9. la campana	9. bell
10. la lectura	10. reading
11. la materia	11. subject
12. el arte	12. art

Conversación

1. Buenos días, muchachos y muchachas.

2. Buenos días, señora Molina.

3. Niños, necesito sus tareas.

4. Aquí está mi tarea, señora Molina.

5. Gracias. Ahora, niños, vamos a estudiar las matemáticas. Catalina, favor de hacer el problema número uno en el pizarrón.

6. Sí, maestra, es 367 por 52. Yo puedo hacer la multiplicación bien.

7. Ya es tiempo para el recreo. Vamos a formar fila. Algunos niños pueden jugar al fútbol y los otros pueden brincar la cuerda.

8. Ahora, muchachos y muchachas, es tiempo para la lectura.

9. ¡Señora Molina, esa es mi materia favorita!

10. ¡Bien! Tenemos una hora antes del almuerzo. Después del almuerzo vamos a estudiar arte.

Conversation

1. Good morning, boys and girls.

2. Good morning, Mrs. Molina.

3. Children, I need your homework.

4. Here is my homework, Mrs. Molina.

5. Thank you. Now, children, let's study our math. Catalina, please do problem number one on the board.

6. Yes, teacher. It's 367 times 52. I'm good at multiplication.

7. Now it's time for recess. Let's line up. Some children can play soccer and others can play jumprope.

8. Now, boys and girls, it's time for reading.

9. Mrs. Molina, that's my favorite subject!

10. Good! We have one hour before lunch. After lunch we will have art.

Historia

Catalina

Catalina es la hija de María y Miguel Ramírez. Ella tiene diez años. Catalina va a la escuela San José. Ella está en cuarto grado. Su maestra es la señora Molina. La materia favorita de Catalina es las matemáticas. Ella multiplica muy bien. En el recreo Catalina juega con Isabel y Anita. Ellas brincan la cuerda. La señora Molina les da tarea a los niños cuatro días a la semana. Ella es una buena maestra. ¡A Catalina le gusta la escuela!

Enrique

Enrique es el hijo de José y Luz García. El tiene once años. Enrique va a la escuela Sierra. El está en quinto grado. Su maestra es la señora Alvarez. A Enrique le gusta la escuela. Es un buen estudiante. Su materia favorita es la lectura. Enrique lee mucho. A Enrique le gusta mucho el recreo. En el recreo él y su amigo, Pablo, juegan al fútbol con los otros niños. Después del recreo la señora Alvarez les lee un cuento a los niños. Luego ellos estudian arte. Enrique tiene facilidad para esta materia. A Enrique le gusta ir a la escuela.

Story

Catalina

Catalina is the daughter of Maria and Miguel Ramirez. She is ten years old. Catalina goes to San Jose School. She is in fourth grade. Her teacher is Mrs. Molina. Catalina's favorite subject is math. She is good at multiplication. At recess Catalina plays with Isabel and Anita. They play jumprope. Mrs. Molina gives the children homework four days a week. She is a good teacher. Catalina likes school!

Enrique

Enrique is the son of Jose and Luz Garcia. He is eleven years old. Enrique goes to Sierra School. He is in fifth grade. His teacher is Mrs. Alvarez. Enrique likes school. He is a good student. His favorite subject is reading. Enrique reads a lot. Enrique really likes recess. At recess he and his friend, Pablo, play soccer with the other children. After recess Mrs. Alvarez reads a story to the children. Then they have art. Enrique is good at art. Enrique likes to go to school.

Fill in the Blank

Fill in the blanks using the vocabulary words. Use each word once.

1. La materia favorita de Catalina son las _____ .

2. La _____ es grande.

3. Catalina escribió el numero uno en el _____ .

4. En el _____ , Enrique juega fútbol con los niños.

5. Catalina puede hacer la _____ bien.

6. Después del almuerzo, los niños estudian

   _____ .

7. La _____ favorita de Enrique es

   la lectura.

8. _____ , niños. Necesito sus tareas.

9. Es tiempo para el recreo. Vamos a _____

   _____ .

10. Ahora, niños, vamos a _____

    las matemáticas.

11. Después del recreo los niños estudian

    la _____ .

12. _____ , niños, vamos a estudiar las matemáticas.

Jumble

Unscramble the vocabulary words.

1. aanmacp _____

2. órnraizp _____

3. ceeror _____

4. tiaream _____

5. radieust _____

6. suenob sída _____

7. tecural _____

8. atámetasicm _____

9. reta _____

10. ipllumcinótica _____

11. morrfa lafi _____

12. roaha _____

buenos días
ahora
estudiar
matemáticas
pizarrón
multiplicación
recreo
formar fila
campana
lectura
materia
arte

Mi Historia

Escriba una historia sobre sí mismo. Incluya: ¿dónde vive?; ¿dónde nació?; ¿qué hace?; ¿cuántos hermanos tiene?; su dirección; y su número de teléfono.

_____

Mi Nombre

Yo vivo en _____

_____

_____

_____

_____

_____

_____

_____

_____

Double Object Pronouns

Many times a direct and indirect object pronoun will appear in the same sentence. When this happens, the indirect object pronoun precedes the direct object pronoun.

Rewrite the following sentences substituting a pronoun for the underlined direct object. The first one has been done for you.

The direct object pronouns in Spanish are *lo, los, la, las*. *Lo* and *los* are masculine pronouns. *La* and *las* are feminine pronouns.

1. El me dio <u>un reloj</u>.

    El me lo dio. _____

2. Su hermana nos dijo <u>un cuento</u>.

    _____

3. Mi mamá te compró <u>unas camisas</u>.

    _____

4. La maestra nos enseñó <u>la lección</u>.

    _____

5. Mi amigo me dio <u>dos perros</u>.

    _____

6. Ella nos dijo <u>la verdad</u>.

    _____

7. ¿Quién te dio <u>el regalo</u>?

    _____

8. Mi abuelo me mandó <u>una carta</u>.

    _____

Answer Key

Fill in the Blank (page 76)

1.	matemáticas	7.	materia
2.	campana	8.	Buenos diás
3.	pizarrón	9.	formar fila
4.	recreo	10.	estudiar
5.	multiplicación	11.	lectura
6.	arte	12.	Ahora

Jumble (page 77)

1.	campana	7.	lectura
2.	pizarrón	8.	matemáticas
3.	recreo	9.	arte
4.	materia	10.	multiplicación
5.	estudiar	11.	formar fila
6.	buenos días	12.	ahora

Mi Historia (page 78)

Mary Smith

Yo vivo en Los Angeles. Nací en Long Beach, California. Soy doctora. Tengo dos hermanos y una hermana. Mi dirección es 564 Bellview Avenue, Los Angeles. Mi número de teléfono es (213) 959-6674.

Double Object Pronouns (page 79)

1. El me lo dio.
2. Su hermana nos lo dijo.
3. Mi mamá te las compró.
4. La maestra nos la enseñó.
5. Mi amigo me los dio.
6. Ella nos la dijo.
7. ¿Quién te lo dio?
8. Mi abuelo me la mandó.

Lección 11 Manejando un Carro
Lesson 11 Driving a Car

Lista de Vocabulario	Vocabulary List
1. conducir	1. to drive
2. la licencia	2. license
3. obtener	3. to get
4. el Departamento de Vehículos Motorizados	4. Department of Motor Vehicles (DMV)
5. las llaves	5. keys
6. el examen	6. test; exam
7. el tráfico	7. traffic
8. el camino	8. road
9. la señal	9. sign
10. aprender	10. to learn
11. la gasolina	11. gasoline
12. la gasolinera	12. gas station

Conversación

1. José, necesito una licencia de manejar. ¿Obtendrás el nuevo Manual del Automovilista de California para mí?

2. Aquí lo tienes, Luz. Me fui al Departamento de Vehículos Motorizados.

3. Gracias, veo que el Manual está en español. Empezaré a estudiarlo hoy.

4. El hombre dijo que tú tienes que tomar tres exámenes: el examen de la vista, un examen escrito, y un examen de conducir.

5. ¡Caramba! Eso es mucho. Verdaderamente tendré que estudiar.

6. El hombre también dijo que tú puedes tomar el examen escrito en español.

7. ¿Me ayudarás a aprender a manejar?

8. Sí, hay mucho que aprender. ¡Vámonos!

Conversation

1. Jose, I need a driver's license. Will you get the new California Driver's Handbook for me?

2. Here it is, Luz. I went to the Department of Motor Vehicles.

3. Thanks, I see the handbook is in Spanish. I'll start studying it today.

4. The man said you have to take three tests: an eye test, a written exam, and a driving test.

5. Wow! That's a lot. I'll really have to study.

6. The man also said you can take the written exam in Spanish.

7. Will you help me learn to drive?

8. Yes, there's a lot to learn. Let's go!

Historia

Un Viaje al Departamento de Vehículos Motorizados

Luz, la esposa de José, quería obtener la licencia de conducir. Primero, ella estudió su Manual del Automovilista. Después ella fue al DMV. Allá ella tuvo que llenar algunos papeles. Le costó doce dólares obtener su licencia de conducir. El primer examen era un examen de la vista. Luz pasó el examen de la vista. Después ella tuvo que tomar un examen acerca de las leyes de tráfico y las señales del camino. Luz pasó ese examen también. Luego Luz tuvo que tomar el examen de conducir. Ella tuvo que usar el carro de José. Luz no quería tomar el examen de conducir porque tuvo que tomarlo en inglés. Un hombre estaba en el carro con Luz. El la observaba con cuidado. Luz lo hizo bien. El DMV le dio a Luz su licencia de conducir. Entonces José y Luz se fueron a cenar a un restaurante.

Story

A Trip to the Department of Motor Vehicles

Luz, Jose's wife, wanted to get a driver's license. First, she studied her Driver's Handbook. Then she went to the DMV. There she had to fill out papers. It cost twelve dollars to get a license. The first test was an eye test. Luz passed the eye test. Then she had to take a test about the traffic laws and road signs. Luz passed that test too. Then Luz had to take the driving test. She had to use Jose's car. Luz did not want to take the driving test because she had to take it in English. A man was in the car with Luz. He watched Luz carefully. Luz did well. The DMV gave Luz her driver's license. Then Jose and Luz went out to eat.

Fill in the Blank

Fill in the blanks using the vocabulary words. Use each word once.

1. José compró _____ para el carro.

2. Luz fue al _____
   para obtener su licencia de conducir.

3. Luz tiene que tomar un _____
   de la vista en el Departamento de Vehículos
   Motorizados.

4. Después ella tuvo que tomar un examen acerca de
   las leyes de tráfico, tuvo que tomar un examen de
   señales del _____ .

5. José fue a la _____ para
   comprar gasolina.

6. Luz no puede manejar un carro hasta que obtenga
   una licencia de _____.

7. Ella quiere _____ una licencia de conducir.

8. El Departamento de Vehículos Motorizados da un
   examen trata de las leyes de _____.

9. Luz quiere _____ como manejar
   un carro.

10. Luz obtiene su _____ de conducir.

11. Luz tiene que tomar un examen de las
    _____ de camino.

12. ¿Dónde están mis _____ ?

Jumble

Unscramble the vocabulary words.

1. ñelas _____		conducir
2. bonetre _____		licencia
3. namoci _____		obtener
4. esaoglarin _____		llaves
5. diccorun _____		examen
6. mxeena _____		tráfico
7. pernarde _____		camino
8. sevlal _____		señal
9. fácrito _____		aprender
10. canecili _____		gasolina
11. lnsaogai _____		gasolinera

Double Object Pronouns

The indirect object pronouns *le* and *les* change to *se* when used with the direct object pronouns *lo, los, la, las*.

Rewrite the following sentences substituting pronouns for the indirect and direct objects.

Example: Ella compró los zapatos para el bebé.
Ella se los compró.

1. Mi mamá dio una muñeca bonita a mi hermana.

   _____

2. Mi abuelo leyó un cuento a los niños.

   _____

3. Yo escribo unas cartas a mis amigas.

   _____

4. Catalina y Carmen explicaron el juego a sus amigas.

   _____

5. Mis abuelos compraron juguetes para mis hijos.

   _____

6. Mi tía mandó unas camisas a mi papá.

   _____

7. Nosotros damos una pelota a los niños.

   _____

8. Mis padres dieron un carro nuevo a mi hermano.

   _____

Days of the Week

Spanish	English
domingo	Sunday
lunes	Monday
martes	Tuesday
miércoles	Wednesday
jueves	Thursday
viernes	Friday
sábado	Saturday

In Spanish, the days of the week are not capitalized. When the definite article (*el, la, los, las*) is used with a day of the week it means *on.*

Write the following sentences in Spanish.

1. Enrique works after school on Tuesdays.

   _____

2. On Fridays my family goes to the movies.

   _____

3. On Sunday Jose goes to church.

   _____

4. Catalina plays soccer on Wednesdays.

   _____

5. On Saturday the children watch cartoons on television.

   _____

6. On Monday my grandmother goes to the doctor.

   _____

7. On Thursday Maria visits her mother.

   _____

Answer Key

Fill in the Blank (page 84)

1. gasolina
2. Departamento de Vehículos Motorizados
3. examen
4. camino
5. gasolinera
6. conducir
7. obtener
8. tráfico
9. aprender
10. licencia
11. señales
12. llaves

Jumble (page 85)

1. señal
2. obtener
3. camino
4. gasolinera
5. conducir
6. examen
7. aprender
8. llaves
9. tráfico
10. licencia
11. gasolina

Double Object Pronouns (page 86)

1. Mi mamá se la dio.
2. Mi abuelo se lo leyó.
3. Yo se las escribo.
4. Catalina y Carmen se lo explicaron.
5. Mis abuelos se los compraron.
6. Mi tía se las mandó.
7. Nosotros se la damos.
8. Mis padres se lo dieron.

Days of the Week (page 87)

1. Enrique trabaja después de la escuela los martes.
2. Los viernes mi familia va al cine.
3. El domingo José va a la iglesia.
4. Catalina juega fútbol los miércoles.
5. El sábado los niños miran las caricaturas en la televisión.
6. El lunes mi abuela va al doctor.
7. El jueves María visita su mamá.

Lección 12 Una Visita a la Tienda de Abarrotes
Lesson 12 A Visit to the Grocery Store

Lista de Vocabulario   Vocabulary List

	Lista de Vocabulario	Vocabulary List
1.	la tienda	store
2.	los abarrotes	groceries
3.	la chequera	checkbook
4.	comprar	to buy
5.	el pollo	chicken
6.	la manzana	apple
7.	la uva	grape
8.	la cebolla	onion
9.	la zanahoria	carrot
10.	la sandía	watermelon
11.	la temporada	season
12.	la margarina	margarine
13.	la harina	flour
14.	el cupón	coupon

Conversación

1. José, tengo que ir a la tienda de abarrotes. ¿Tienes la chequera?

2. Sí, Luz, aquí la tienes. ¿Vas a llevar a Antonio?

3. Sí, él siempre se porta bien en la tienda. Tengo mi lista y la chequera.

4. Me voy al departamento de carnes primero. Necesito hamburguesa, tocino, pollo, y pescado.

5. Ahora, compraré las frutas y las legumbres. ¿Señor Vasconcelos, la sandía es de la temporada?

6. No, tendremos sandías la próxima semana, señora García.

7. Bien. Ahora, necesito la leche, la margarina, la harina, y los huevos.

8. ¡Hola! Aquí están los cupones.

9. Señora García, eso será $101.59.

10. Aquí está mi cheque por $125.00.

11. ¡Gracias! Aquí tiene su cambio.

Conversation

1. Jose, I have to go to the grocery store. Do you have the checkbook?

2. Yes, Luz, here it is. Are you going to take Antonio?

3. Yes, he's always good at the store. I have my list and the checkbook.

4. I'll go to the meat department first. I need hamburger, bacon, chicken, and fish.

5. Now, I'll get the fruits and vegetables. Mr. Vasconcelos, is watermelon in season yet?

6. No, we will have watermelon next week, Mrs. Garcia.

7. O.K. Now I need milk, margarine, flour, and eggs.

8. Hi! Here's my coupons.

9. Mrs. Garcia, that will be $101.59.

10. Here is my check for $125.00.

11. Thank you! Here is your change.

Historia

Una Visita a la Tienda 7-11

Luz estaba haciendo la cena. Ella necesitaba algunas cosas de la tienda. Luz le pidió a Enrique que fuera a la tienda 7-11. Enrique estaba jugando con su amigo Pablo. El no quería ir de compras pero Luz dijo que le daba $1.00. Enrique fue a la tienda 7-11. Su amigo Pablo fue con él. Enrique compró algunos plátanos, cebollas, la margarina, y la harina. El le dio a la mujer diez dólares. La mujer le dio $3.67 de cambio. Enrique compró el helado para él y para Pablo. Los dos muchachos fueron a la casa. Enrique le dio a su mamá los abarrotes. Entonces, Luz terminaba haciendo la cena.

Story

A Visit to the 7-11 Store

Luz was making dinner. She needed some things at the store. Luz asked Enrique to go to the 7-11 Store. Enrique was playing with his friend Pablo. He did not want to go shopping but Luz said she would give him $1.00. Enrique went to the 7-11 Store. His friend Pablo went with him. Enrique bought some bananas, onions, margarine, and flour. He gave the woman ten dollars. The woman gave him $3.67 in change. Enrique bought ice cream for himself and for Pablo. The two boys walked home. Enrique gave the groceries to his mother. Then Luz finished making dinner.

Fill in the Blank

Fill in the blanks using the vocabulary words. Use each word once.

1. María dio sus _____ a la mujer en la tienda.

2. La _____ es una fruta que es roja, verde, y blanca.

3. María necesita su _____ para pagar por los abarrotes.

4. Enrique fue a la _____ 7-11.

5. En el departamento de carne María compró _____ .

6. Una _____ es una fruta roja.

7. El verano es la _____ para la sandía .

8. Una _____ es una legumbre. Es del mismo color de una naranja.

9. María usará _____ para hacer pan.

10. Mi tío no le pone _____ al pan tostado.

11. Enrique dio a la mujer diez dólares para los

    _____ .

12. María necesita manzanas, naranjas, bananas, y

    _____ del departamento de fruta.

13. Ella _____ abarrotes en el mercado.

14. A Pablo le gusta la _____ en su hamburguesa.

Negative Sentences

In Spanish the most common way to make a negative sentence is to place the word *no* in front of the verb. If there is an object pronoun before the verb, the negative word is placed before the object pronoun.

Examples: Catalina va a la tienda.
Catalina no va a la tienda.

A José le gusta el pollo.
A José no le gusta el pollo.

Rewrite the following sentences in the negative.

1. Las naranjas están en temporada.

   _____

2. A Carmen le gustan las uvas.

   _____

3. Yo tengo mi chequera.

   _____

4. Enrique lo dijo.

   _____

5. Mi amiga y yo compramos boletos para el cine.

   _____

6. Mi tía tiene muchos cupones.

   _____

7. Mi hermano le pone jalea al pan.

   _____

8. A los niños les gusta la sandía.

   _____

Verb Practice

dormir - to sleep

In Spanish, it is the ending of the verb that indicates the doer of the action.

Spanish		English	
Pronoun	Verb	Pronoun	Verb
yo	duermo	I	sleep
tú	duermes	you	sleep
él, ella, usted	duerme	he, she; you	sleeps; sleep
nosotros	dormimos	we	sleep
ellos, ellas, ustedes	duermen	they, you *(plural)*	sleep

Write the following sentences in Spanish.

1. They sleep in a big bed.

   _____

2. The baby sleeps in the afternoon.

   _____

3. My grandfather sleeps a lot.

   _____

4. On Fridays we sleep at my grandmother's house.

   _____

5. I sleep eight hours every night.

   _____

6. You sleep in a pretty bedroom.

   _____

7. She sleeps in a small bed.

   _____

Contractions

There are only two contractions in Spanish. They are *al* and *del*. *Al* is the contraction of the preposition *a* (to) and the definite article *el*. *Del* is the contraction of the preposition *de* (of, from, about) and the definite article *el*. There are no contractions with feminine or plural articles.

Complete the following sentences with either *al* or *del*.

1. **Nosotros vamos** _____ **mercado.**

2. **La fotografía** _____ **perro es chistosa.**

3. **Ellos quieren ir** _____ **cine.**

4. **La vista** _____ **pueblo es bonita.**

5. **Es la hija** _____ **señor García.**

Complete the following sentences. The first one has been done for you.

6. **A mi me gusta mucho la vista** ____*de las*____ **montañas.**

7. **Nosotros vamos** _____ **parque.**

8. **La comida** _____ **gato está en la cocina.**

9. **Mi hermana va** _____ **tienda.**

10. **Los juguetes** _____ **niños están sucios.**

11. **Mi familia va** _____ **playa en el verano.**

12. **En el invierno nosotros vamos** _____ **desierto.**

13. **Son los hijos** _____ **señora Ramírez.**

14. **Jorge va** _____ **juego de fútbol.**

15. **Los ojos** _____ **bebé son azules.**

Answer Key

Fill in the Blank (page 92)

1. cupones
2. sandía
3. chequera
4. tienda
5. pollo
6. manzana
7. temporada
8. zanahoria
9. harina
10. margarina
11. abarrotes
12. uvas
13. compra
14. cebolla

Negative Sentences (page 93)

1. Las naranjas no están en temporada.
2. A Carmen no le gustan las uvas.
3. Yo no tengo mi chequera.
4. Enrique no lo dijo.
5. Mi amiga y yo no compramos boletos para el cine.
6. Mi tía no tiene muchos cupones.
7. Mi hermano no le pone jalea al pan.
8. A los niños no les gusta la sandía.

Verb Practice (page 94)

1. Ellos duermen en una cama grande.
2. El bebé duerme en la tarde.
3. Mi abuelo duerme mucho.
4. Los viernes dormimos en la casa de mi abuela.
5. Yo duermo ocho horas cada noche.
6. Tú duermes en una recámara bonita.
7. Ella duerme en una cama pequeña.

Contractions (page 95)

1. al
2. del
3. al
4. del
5. del

6. de las
7. al
8. del
9. a la
10. de los
11. a la
12. al
13. de la
14. al
15. del

Dictionary

Spanish – English

A

a - to, on
abajo - below
abarrotes - groceries
abuela - grandmother
abuelo - grandfather
acerca de - about
acostarse - to go to bed
adelante - forward; ahead
adiós - good-bye
aeroplano - airplane
afuera - out; outside
ahora - now
al [a + el] - to the
algún(o) - some
allá - there; over there
almuerzo - lunch
alto(a) - high; loud
amar - to love
    amo - I love
amarillo - yellow
americano - American
amigo - friend
anaranjado - orange
andar - to walk
antes - before
añadir - to add
año - year
aprender - to learn
apurarse - to hurry up
aquel, aquello - that one
aquellos - those

aquí- here
arte - art
avión - airplane
ayuda - help
ayudar - to help
azúcar - sugar
azul - blue

B

bahía - bay
bandera - flag
baño - bath
barco - boat
bebé - baby
beber - to drink
beisbol - baseball
beso - kiss
bien - fine; O.K.
bistec - steak
blanco - white
boca - mouth
boleto - ticket
bonito - pretty
brincar - to jump
    brincar la cuerda - to jump rope
buen(o) - good
    buenos días - good morning

C

cabeza - head

cada - each; every
café - brown; coffee
calle - street
cama - bed
cambiar – to change
cambio - change
camino - road
camisa - shirt
campana - bell
campo - field
caricaturas - cartoons
carne - meat
carro - car
carta - letter
casa - house
    casa de muñecas - dollhouse
catarro - cold
cazar - to hunt
cebolla - onion
celebrar - to celebrate
cena - dinner
cenar - to have dinner
    cena - he/she has dinner
    cenas - you have dinner
cepillar - to brush
cerca - nearby
cerveza - beer
cien - one hundred
cinco - five
cincuenta - fifty
cine - movie
cita - appointment; date
ciudad - city
cocina - kitchen
color - color
comer - to eat
    como - I eat
    comes - you eat
    come - he/she eats
    comemos - we eat

    coméis - you (plural) eat
    comen - they eat
comida - meal
comió - he/she ate
como - as; like
¿cómo? - how?
compra - purchase
comprar - to buy
    compramos - we buy
    compraron - they bought
    compró - he/she bought
con - with
    con cuidado - carefully
conducir - to drive
conductor - driver
conocer - to meet; to know
conversación - conversation
corte - court
cosa - thing
costar - to cost
costoso - expensive
crema - cream
cual - which
¿cuál? - which one?; what?
cuando - when
¿cuándo? - when?
¿cuánto? - how much?
¿cuántos? - how many?
cuarto - fourth
cuatro - four
cuento - story, tale
cuerda - rope
cuerpo - body
cuidado - care
cupón - coupon

Ch

cheque - check
chequera - checkbook

chistoso(a) - funny
chocolate - chocolate

D

dar - to give
   doy - I give
   das - you give
   da - he/she gives
   damos - we give
   dais - you (plural) give
   dan - they give
de - of; from
   de veras - truly
deber - to have to
decidir - to decide
decir - to say; to tell
declarar - to declare
del [de + el] - of the
delicioso - delicious
departamento - department
depender - to depend
derecha - right side
desayuno - breakfast
desierto - desert
después - after; afterwards
di - I gave
día - day
   día de fiesta - holiday
dientes - teeth
dieron - they gave
diez - ten
difícil - difficult
dijo - he/she said
dinero - money
dio - he/she gave
Dios - God
dirección - address
distinto - different

doble - double
doctor - doctor
dólar - dollar
domingo - Sunday
donde - where
¿dónde? - where?
dormir - to sleep
   duermo - I sleep
   duermes - you sleep
   duerme - he/she sleeps
   dormimos - they sleep
   dormís - you (plural) sleep
   duermen - they sleep
dos - two
durante - during
durar - to last
duro - hard

E

edificio - building
ejemplo - example
ejercicio - exercise
el - the
él - he
ella - she
ello - it
ellos - they
empezar - to start
en - in; on
   en adelante - from now on
enamorado - boyfriend
encontrar - to find
enfermo - sick
enfrente - in front
enseñar - to show; to teach
enseñó - he/she taught; he/she
   showed
entonces - then

entre - between
equivale - to be equivalent
era - he/she/it was
eran - they were
escribió - he/she wrote
escribir – to write
escuela - school
ese - that
eso - that
espacio - space
español - Spanish
esposa - wife
estación - season
estado - state
estar - to be
    estoy - I am
    estás - you are
    está - he/she/it is
    estamos - we are
    estáis - you(plural) are
    están - they are
esto - this
estrella - star
estudiante - student
estudiar - to study
exacto - exact
examen - test; exam
examinar - to examine
excelente - excellent

F

familia - family
favor - favor
    favor de - please
favorito - favorite
feliz - happy
fiebre - fever
fiesta - holiday
fila - row

100

fin - end
final - final
forma - form; shape
formar - to form
    formar fila - to line up
fotografía - photograph
franja - stripe
frío - cold
fruta - fruit
fue - he/she/it went
fuiste - you went
fútbol - soccer
futuro - future

G

galón - gallon
ganso - goose
gasolina - gasoline
gasolinera - gas station
gato - cat
gente - people
gobierno - government
gracias - thanks; thank you
grado - degree; grade
grande - big
gripe - flu
guardar cama - to stay in bed
guerra - war
gustar - to like

H

hablar - to speak; to talk
    hablo - I speak
    hablas - you speak
    habla - he/she speaks
    hablamos - we speak

h_bláis - you (plural) speak
hablan - they speak
hacer - to do; to make
hamburguesa - hamburger
harina - flour
hasta - until
hay - there is; there are
    hay que - it is necessary
hecho - made
helado - ice cream
hermana - sister
hermano - brother
hija - daughter
hijo - son
historia - history; story
hola - hello
hombre - man
hora - hour
hotel - hotel
hoy - today
huevo - egg

I

iglesia - church
igual - equal
iguales - matching
incluya - include
indicar - to indicate
indio - Indian
inglés - English
interesante - interesting
invierno - winter
ir - to go
    voy - I go
    vas - you go
    va - he/she/it goes
    vamos - we go
    vais - you (plural) go
    van - they go

ir de compras - to go shopping
irse - to go away

J

jalea - jelly
jefe - chief
juega - he/she plays
juego - game
jueves - Thursday
jugar - to play
    jugando - playing
jugo - juice
juguete - toy

K

L

la - the
le - him, her, you; to him, to her,
    to you
lección - lesson
leche - milk
lechuga - lettuce
lectura - reading
leer - to read
legumbre - vegetable
levantarse - to get up; me
    levanto - I get up
ley - law
libra - pound
libreta - notebook
libro - book
licencia - license

licencia de manejar - driver's license
limpiar - to clean
lista - list
lo - him, you, it
    lo cual - that which
luego - soon
lugar - place
lunes - Monday

LL

llamar - to call; to name
    llamar por teléfono - to telephone
llamarse - to be called; me llamo - my name is
llave - key
llegar - to come
llenar - to fill; to fill out
    llene el espacio - fill in the blank
llevar - to bring

M

madre - mother
maestro - teacher
mamá - mom
mandó - he/she sent
manejar - to drive
manera - manner; way
mano - hand
manual - manual; handbook
manzana - apple
mañana - morning; tomorrow
margarina - margarine
martes - Tuesday

más - more
matemáticas - mathematics; math
materia - subject
mayor - older
me - me
medicina - medicine
mejor - better
memoria - memory
menor - younger
mercado - market
mesa - table
mi - my
miércoles - Wednesday
mío - my; mine
mirar - to look
mismo - self
mitad - half
montañas - mountains
morado - purple
morir - to die
motor - motor
muchacha - girl
muchacho - boy
mucho - much; a lot
muchos - many
mudarse - to move
mujer - woman
multiplicación - multiplication
multiplicar - to multiply
muñeca - doll
muy - very

N

nací - I was born
nadar - to swim
naranja - orange
nariz - nose
náusea - nausea

necesitar - to need
    necesita - he/she/it needs
negro - black
ni - neither
nieve - snow
niño - child; boy
niños - children
no - no
noche - night
nombrar - to name
nombre - name
nosotros - we
notar - to note; to observe
nuestro - our
nueve - nine
nuevo - new
número - number

Ñ

O

o - or
observar - to observe
obtener - to get
ocho - eight
oficina - office
oído - ear
ojo - eye
oración - sentence
otro - another

P

padre - father
pagar - to pay

país - country
pan - bread
    pan tostado - toast
papa - potato
papá - dad
papel - paper
para - for; to; toward; in order to
parque - park
parte - part
pasar - to pass
    pasar lista - to call roll
pavo - turkey
pegar - to hit
pelo - hair
pelota - ball
pensar - to think
pequeño - little
permitir - to permit; to let
pero - but
perro - dog
persona - person
pescado - fish
pie - foot
pizarrón - board; blackboard
plátano - banana
playa - beach
poco - little
pollo - chicken
poner - to put
    pongo - I put
    pones - you put
    pone - he/she/it puts
    ponemos - we put
    ponéis - you (plural) put
    ponen - they put
ponerse - to put on
popular - popular
por - for; times
    por favor - please
¿por qué? - why?

porque - because
portarse - to behave
practicar - to practice
pregunta - question
preparar - to prepare
primer(o) - first
próximo - next
pueblo - town

Q

que - that
¿qué? - what?
quedarse - to stay
querer - to want
    quiero - I want
    quieres - you want
    quiere - he/she wants
    queremos - we want
    queréis - you (plural) want
    quieren - they want
¿quién? - who?
quítalo - take it out
quitar - to take away
quitarse - to take off

R

ratón - mouse
raya - line
realidad (en) - really
recámara - bedroom
recordar - to remember
recreo - recess
regalo - gift
regla - rule
regresar - to return
religión - religion

reloj - clock; watch
restaurante - restaurant
reunirse - to meet
roca - rock
rojo - red
ropa - clothes; clothing

RR

S

sábado - Saturday
saber - to know
salir - to go out; to leave
sandía - watermelon
segundo - second
seis - six
semana - week
sentarse - to sit down
sentido - meaning
sentirse - to feel
señal - sign
señor - Mr.
señora - Mrs.
señorita - Miss
ser - to be
    soy - I am
    eres - you are
    es - he/she/it is
    somos - we are
    sois - you (plural) are
    son - they are
servir - to serve
si - if
sí - yes
    sí mismo - himself
siempre - always

siete - seven
simpático - nice
simplemente - simply
sin - without
sobre - over; on
solamente - only
sombrero - hat
sonar - to ring
sonido - sound
sopa - soup
su - your, his, her, its, their
sucio - dirty
supermercado - supermarket

T

taco - taco
también - also
tampoco - either
tarde - afternoon
tarea - job; homework
tarjeta - card
taza - cup
te - you
té - tea
telefonear - to telephone
teléfono - telephone
televisión - television
temperatura - temperature
temporada - season
temprano - early
tener - to have
    tengo- I have
    tienes - you have
    tiene - he/she/it has
    tenemos - we have
    tenéis - you (plura) have
    tienen - they have

tener que - to have to
tercero - third
terminación - end
terminar - to finish
tía - aunt
tiempo - time
tienda - store
tío - uncle
tocar - to touch
tocino - bacon
todo - all
tomar - to take; to drink
    tomo - I take; drink
    tomas - you take; drink
    toma - he/she takes; drinks
    tomamos - we take; drink
    tomáis - you (plural) take; drink
    toman - we take; drink
tomate - tomato
tostado - toasted
trabajar - to work
trabajo - work
traducir - to translate
traer - to bring; to take
traje - suit
    traje de baño - bathing suit
trece - thirteen
tres - three
tu - your
tú - you
tuvo - he/she/it had

U

un(a) - a, an
uno - one
usar - to use
usará - he/she will use
usted - you

usualmente - usually
uva - grape

V

vehículo - vehicle
venir - to come
ver - to see
verano - summer
verdad - truth
verdaderamente - really
verde - green
vestido - dress
viajar - to travel
viaje - trip
viernes - Friday
visita - visit
visitar - to visit
vista - view
vivir - to live
    vivo - I live
    vives - you live
    vive - he/she lives
    vivimos - we live
    vivís - you (plural) live
    viven - they live
vocabulario - vocabulary
vosotros - you (plural)
voto - vote
voy - I go; me voy a - I am going
    to
voz - voice

W

X

Y

y - and
ya - already
yo - I

Z

zapato – shoe

Dictionary

English – Spanish

A

a - un, una
about - casi
address - dirección
after - después
afternoon - tarde
airplane - avión
all - todo
also - también
always - siempre; todo el tiempo
American - americano
an - un, una
and - y
answer - respuesta
any - alguno; ninguno
anything - alguna cosa
apple - manzana
appointment - cita
art - arte
as - como
at - en
aunt - tía

B

baby - bebé
bacon - tocino
ball - pelota
banana - plátano

baseball - beisbol

bathing suit - traje de baño
bay - bahía
be (to) - ser ; estar
beach - playa
because - porque
bed - cama
bedroom - recámara
beer - cerveza
before - antes
behave (to) - portarse
bell - campana
belong to (to) - pertenecer
better - mejor
big - grande
black - negro
blacker - más negro
blackest - el más negro
blank - espacio
blue - azul
bluer - más azul
bluest - el más azul
board (blackboard) - pizarrón
boat - barco
body - cuerpo
book - libro
boy - muchacho
bread - pan
breakfast - desayuno
bring (to) - llevar; traer
brother - hermano
brown - café
browner - más café

brownest - el más café
brush (to) - cepillar
building - edificio
but - pero
buy (to) - comprar
    buying - comprando
by - por

C

call (to) - llamar
    call roll (to) - pasar lista
car - carro
card - tarjeta
carefully - con cuidado
carrot - zanahoria
cartoons - caricaturas
cat - gato
celebrate (to) - celebrar
cereal - cereal
change - cambio
check - cheque
checkbook - chequera
chicken - pollo
child - niño
children - niños
chocolate - chocolate
church - iglesia
clean - limpio
cleaner - más limpio
cleanest - el más limpio
clock - reloj
clothes - ropa
coffee - café
cold - catarro; frio
colder - más frío
coldest - el más frío
color - color

come (to) - venir; llegar
conversation - conversación
cost (to) - costar
country - país
coupon - cupón
cream - crema
cup - taza

D

dad - papá
daughter - hija
day - día
decide (to) - decidir
declare (to) - declarar
deer - venado
delicious - delicioso
department - departamento
depend (to) - depender
desert - desierto
die (to) - morir
difficult - difícil
dinner - cena
dirty - sucio
do (to) - hacer
doctor - doctor
dog - perro
dollar - dólar
dress - vestido
drink (to) - beber, tomar
drive (to) - manejar; conducir
driver - conductor
    driver's license - licencia de
    manejar
during - durante

E

each - cada
ear - oído
early - temprano
eat (to) - comer
    eating - comiendo
egg - huevo
eight - ocho
either - tampoco
else - otro
every - cada
everything - todo
exam - examen
examine (to) - examinar
excellent - excelente
expensive - costoso
eye - ojo

F

family - familia
father -padre
favorite - favorito
feel (to) - sentirse
fever - fiebre
field - campo
fifty - cincuenta
fine - bien; fino
finer - más fino
finest - el más fino
first - primero
fish - pescado
five - cinco
flag - bandera
flour - harina
flu - influenza
food -comida
foot - pie
for - por; para
found (to) - fundar

four - cuatro
Friday - viernes
friend - amigo
from - de
fruit - fruta
funny - chistoso(a)

G

gallon - galón
game - juego
gas station - gasolinera
gasoline - gasolina
geese - gansos
get (to) - obtener
    get up (to) - subirse; levantarse
gift - regalo
girl - muchacha
give (to) - dar
    giving - dando
go (to) - ir
    going - yendo
    go to bed - acostarse
God - Dios
good - bueno
    good morning - buenos días
good-bye - adiós
goose - ganso
grade - grado
grandfather - abuelo
grandmother - abuela
grape - uva
green - verde
greener - más verde
greenest - el más verde
groceries - abarrotes
grocery store - tienda de abarrotes
grow (to) - cultivar

H

hair - pelo
half - mitad
hamburger - hamburguesa
hand - mano
handbook - manual
happy - feliz
hat - sombrero
have (to) - tener
    have to (to) - tener que
he - él
    he is - está; es
    he does - hace
    he eats - come
    he goes - va
    he has - tiene
    he lives - vive
    he plays - juega
    he sleeps - duerme
    he studies - estudia
    he watches - mira
    he works - trabaja
head - cabeza
hello! - ¡hola!
help (to) - ayudar
her - su, sus
here - aquí
hi! - ¡hola!
high - alto
higher - más alto
highest - el más alto
him - le, lo, o con él
himself - él mismo
his - su, sus
hit (to) - pegar
holiday - día de fiesta
home - el hogar
homework - tarea
110

hotel - hotel
hour - hora
house - casa
how? - ¿cómo?
    how many? - ¿cuántos?
    how much? - ¿cuánto?
hunt (to) - cazar
hurry (to) - apurarse

I

I - yo
    I am - soy; estoy
    I do - hago
    I eat - como
    I go - voy
    I have - tengo
    I live - vivo
    I play - juego
    I sleep - duermo
    I study - estudio
    I watch - miro
    I work - trabajo
ice cream - helado
if - si
in - en
interesting - interesante
it - ello
it's - ello es
its - de ello

J

jelly - jalea
join - juntarse
juice - jugo
jumprope - cuerda para brincar

K

key - llave
kiss - beso
kitchen - cocina
know (to) - saber

L

later - más tarde
learn (to) - aprender
lesson - lección
letter - carta
lettuce - lechuga
license - licencia
like (to) - gustar
line up (to) - formar fila
little - pequeño
littler - más pequeño
littlest - el más pequeño
live (to) - vivir
   living - viviendo
long - largo
lots - muchos
loud - alto
love (to)- amar
lunch - almuerzo

M

make (to) - hacer
   making - haciendo
man - hombre
many - muchos
margarine - margarina

market - mercado
matching - iguales
math - matemáticas
mathematics - matemáticas
me - me; a mí
meat - carne
medicine - medicina
meet (to) - conocer; reunirse
men - hombres
mice - ratones
milk - leche
Miss - señorita
mom - mamá
Monday - lunes
money - dinero
more - más
morning - mañana
mother - madre
motor - motorizado
mountains - montañas
mouse - ratón
mouth - boca
move - mudarse
movie - cine
Mr. - señor
Mrs. - señora
much - mucho
multiplication - multiplicación
my - mi, mis; mío, míos

N

name - nombre
near - cerca
nearby - cerca
need (to) - necesitar
new - nuevo
next - próximo
nice - simpático

night - noche
nine - nueve
no - no
nose - nariz
not - no
now - ahora
number - número

O

o'clock- del reloj
of - de
office - oficina
O.K. - bien; ¡Bueno!
older - mayor
on - en, encima de
one - uno
onion - cebolla
only - solamente
or - o
orange - naranja; anaranjado
order - orden
other - otro
our - nuestro
out - fuera; afuera
own - propio

P

paper - papel
park - parque
part - parte
pass (to) - pasar
pay (to) - pagar
penny - centavo
people - personas
person - persona

photograph - fotografía
place - lugar
play - jugar
   playing - jugando
please - por favor
popular - popular
potato - papa
pretty - bonito
purple - morado
put (to) - poner
   put on (to) - ponerse

Q

question - pregunta

R

read (to) - leer
reading - lectura
really - en realidad
recess - recreo
red - rojo
religion - religión
restaurant - restaurante
return - regresar
Right! - ¡Bien!
ring (to) - sonar
road - camino
rock - roca
room - cuarto
rope - cuerda

S

same - mismo

Saturday - sábado
say (to) - decir
school - escuela
season - estación; temporada
see (to) - ver
sentence - oración
serve (to) - servir
set the table (to) - poner la mesa
seven - siete
she - ella
    she is - está; es
    she does - hace
    she eats - come
    she goes - va
    she has - tiene
    she lives - vive
    she plays - juega
    she sleeps - duerme
    she studies - estudia
    she watches - mira
    she works - trabaja
shirt - camisa
shoe - zapato
sick - enfermo
sicker - más enfermo
sickest - el más enfermo
sign - señal
sister - hermana
sit (to) - sentarse
six - seis
sleep (to) - dormir
    sleeping - durmiendo
small - pequeño
smaller - más pequeño
smallest - el más pequeño
so - entonces
soccer - fútbol
some - alguno; unos
son - hijo
soup - sopa

Spanish - español
star - estrella
start (to) - empezar
state - estado
stay (to) - quedarse
    stay in bed (to) - guardar cama
steak - bistec
stop (to) - detenerse
store - tienda
story - historia; cuento
stripe - franja
student - estudiante
study (to) - estudiar
    studying - estudiando
subject - materia; sujeto
sugar - azúcar
suit - traje
summer - verano
Sunday - domingo
supermarket - supermercado
swim (to) - nadar

T

table - mesa
taco - taco
take (to) - tomar
    take off (to) - quitarse
talk (to) - hablar
tea - té
teacher - maestro
teeth - dientes
telephone - teléfono
television - televisión
tell (to) - decir
temperature - temperatura
ten - diez
test - examen
thank you - gracias
    thanks - gracias

that - ese, eso, aquel
the - el, la, lo, los, las
their - su, sus
them - los, las
then - entonces; luego
there - allá
    there are - hay
therefore - por eso
they - ellos, ellas
    they are - son; están
    they do - hacen
    they eat - comen
    they go - van
    they have - tienen
    they live - viven
    they play - juegan
    they sleep - duermen
    they study - estudian
    they watch - miran
    they work - trabajan
thing - cosa
think (to) - pensar
thirteen - trece
this - este, esta, esto
those - aquellos
three - tres
Thursday - jueves
ticket - boleto
time - hora; tiempo
times - por
to - a
toast - pan tostado
today - hoy
tomato - tomate
tomorrow - mañana
too - también
touch (to) - tocar
town - pueblo
toy - juguete
traffic - tráfico

travel (to) - viajar
trip - viaje
truth - verdad
Tuesday - martes
turkey - pavo
TV - televisión
two - dos

U

uncle - tío
United States - Estados Unidos
until - hasta
up - arriba
use (to) - usar

V

vegetable - legumbre
vehicle - vehículo
verb - verbo
very - muy
view - vista
visit (to) - visitar
visit - visita
vocabulary - vocabulario
voice - voz
vote - voto

W

walk (to) - andar
want (to) - querer
war - guerra
watch - reloj
watch (to) - mirar

watching - mirando
watermelon - sandía
we - nosotros
    we are - somos; estamos
    we do - hacemos
    we eat - comemos
    we go - vamos
    we have - tenemos
    we live - vivimos
    we play - jugamos
    we sleep - dormimos
    we study - estudiamos
    we watch - miramos
    we work - trabajamos
Wednesday - miércoles
week - semana
well! - ¡bueno!
what - lo que
    what? - ¿qué?; ¿cuál?
when - cuando
    when? - ¿cuándo?
where - donde
    where? - ¿dónde?
which - lo que; lo cual
    which? - ¿cuál?
white - blanco
whiter - más blanco
whitest - el más blanco
who - quien
    who? - ¿quién?; ¿quiénes?
why? - ¿por qué?
wife - esposa
winter - invierno
with - con
woman - mujer
women - mujeres
work - trabajo
work (to) - trabajar
    working - trabajando
wow! - ¡caramba!

write (to) - escribir

X

Y

year - año
yellow - amarillo
yellower - más amarillo
yellowest - el más amarillo
yes - sí
yet - ya
you - tú, usted
    you are - eres, es; estás, está
    you do - haces; hace
    you eat - comes; come
    you go - vas; va
    you have - tienes; tiene
    you live - vives; vive
younger - menor
your - tu, tus, su, sus

Z

Index

Books Available From **FISHER HILL**
For Ages 10-Adult

ENGLISH READING COMPREHENSION FOR THE SPANISH SPEAKER Book 1

ENGLISH READING AND SPELLING FOR THE SPANISH SPEAKER Books 1, 2, 3, 4, 5 & 6

ENGLISH for the SPANISH SPEAKER Books 1, 2, 3, 4 & Cassettes

SPANISH made FUN and EASY Books 1 & 2

HEALTH Easy to Read

UNITED STATES OF AMERICA Stories, Maps, Activities in Spanish and English Books 1, 2, 3, & 4

English Reading Comprehension for the Spanish Speaker Book 1 contains twenty lessons to help Spanish-speaking students improve their reading comprehension skills. Each lesson includes two vocabulary pages, a visualization page, a fluency page, two comprehension skill pages, and an answer key. This is an excellent book to use after completing *English Reading and Spelling for the Spanish Speaker Book 1*. Price is $15.95, size is 8 1/2 x11 and 161 pages. ISBN 1-878253-37-9.

English Reading and Spelling for the Spanish Speaker Books 1, 2, 3, 4, 5 & 6 contain twenty lessons to help Spanish-speaking students learn to read and spell English. The books use a systematic approach in teaching the English speech sounds and other phonological skills. They also present basic sight words that are not phonetic. The word lists are in Spanish and English and all directions are in Spanish with English translations. Each book is $14.95 and approximately 142 pages. Book size is 8 1/2 x 11. Book 1 ISBN 1-878253-24-7, Book 2 ISBN 1-878253-25-5, Book 3 ISBN 1-878253-26-3, Book 4 ISBN 1-878253-29-8, Book 5 ISBN 1-878253-30-1, Book 6 ISBN 1-878253-35-2.

ENGLISH for the SPANISH SPEAKER Books 1, 2, 3, & 4 are English as a Second Language workbooks for ages 10 - adult. Each book is divided into eight lessons and is written in Spanish and English. Each lesson includes: vocabulary, a conversation, a story, four activity pages, an answer key, two dictionaries: English-Spanish and Spanish-English, a puzzle section, and an index. Each book is $12.95 and approximately 110 pages. Book size is 8 1/2 x 11. Book 1 ISBN 1-878253-07-7, Book 2 ISBN 1-878253-16-6, Book 3 ISBN 1-878253-17-4, Book 4 ISBN 1-878253-18-2; Book 1 Cassette ISBN 1-878253-21-2, Book 2 Cassette ISBN 1-878253-32-8, Book 3 Cassette ISBN 1-878253-33-6, Book 4 Cassette ISBN 1-878253-34-4.

SPANISH made FUN and EASY Books 1 & 2 are workbooks for ages 10 - adult. Each book includes stories, games, conversations, activity pages, vocabulary lists, dictionaries, and an index. The books are for beginning Spanish students; people who want to brush up on high school Spanish; or for Spanish speakers who want to learn how to read and write Spanish. Each book is $14.95 and 134 pages. Book size is 8 1/2 x 11. Book 1 ISBN 1-878253-42-5, Book 2 ISBN 1-878253-19-0.

HEALTH Easy to Read contains 21 easy to read stories. After each story is a vocabulary page, a grammar page, and a question and answer page. The stories are about changing people's life styles to reduce their risk of poor health and premature death. Book is $13.95 and has 118 pages. Book size is 8 1/2 x 11. ISBN 1-878253-41-7. Revised 2005.

United STATES of America Stories, Maps, Activities in SPANISH and ENGLISH Books 1, 2, 3, & 4 are easy to read books about the United States of America for ages 10 - adult. Each state is presented by a story, map, and activities. Each book contains information for 12 to 13 states and has an answer key and index. The states are presented in alphabetical order. Book size is 8 1/2 x 11. Each book is $14.95 and approximately 140 pages.

Book 1 ISBN 1-878253-23-9 Alabama through Idaho
Book 2 ISBN 1-878253-11-5 Illinois through Missouri
Book 3 ISBN 1-878253-12-3 Montana through Pennsylvania
Book 4 ISBN 1-878253-13-1 Rhode Island through Wyoming

ORDER FORM

1. **By Phone:** Call 714-377-9353 or 800-494-4652 8:00 A.M. to 5:00 P.M. Pacific Time. 2. **By Fax:** Fax your order to 714-377-9495.
3. **By Mail:** Send your order to Fisher Hill. 4. **On line:** www.Fisher-Hill.com (Also view sample lessons.)

Name: _____

Address: _____
_____

Purchase Order Number: _____

Credit Card Number and Expiration Date: _____
We accept Visa and Mastercard only.   Please include cardholder's name.

QUANTITY	BOOK TITLE	RETAIL PRICE	AMOUNT
	English Reading Comprehension for the Spanish Speaker Book 1	$15.95	
	English Reading and Spelling for the Spanish Speaker Book 1	$14.95	
	English Reading and Spelling for the Spanish Speaker Book 2	$14.95	
	English Reading and Spelling for the Spanish Speaker Book 3	$14.95	
	English Reading and Spelling for the Spanish Speaker Book 4	$14.95	
	English Reading and Spelling for the Spanish Speaker Book 5	$14.95	
	English Reading and Spelling for the Spanish Speaker Book 6	$14.95	
	Diccionario Español-Inglés	$5.99	
	English For The Spanish Speaker Book 1	$12.95	
	English For The Spanish Speaker Book 1 Cassette	$10.95	
	English For The Spanish Speaker Book 1 and Cassette	$21.95	
	English For The Spanish Speaker Book 2	$12.95	
	English For The Spanish Speaker Book 2 Cassette	$10.95	
	English For The Spanish Speaker Book 2 and Cassette	$21.95	
	English For The Spanish Speaker Book 3	$12.95	
	English For The Spanish Speaker Book 3 Cassette	$10.95	
	English For The Spanish Speaker Book 3 and Cassette	$21.95	
	English For The Spanish Speaker Book 4	$12.95	
	English For The Spanish Speaker Book 4 Cassette	$10.95	
	English For The Spanish Speaker Book 4 and Cassette	$21.95	
	HEALTH Easy to Read	$13.95	
	USA Stories, Maps, Activities in Spanish & English Book 1	$14.95	
	USA Stories, Maps, Activities in Spanish & English Book 2	$14.95	
	USA Stories, Maps, Activities in Spanish & English Book 3	$14.95	
	USA Stories, Maps, Activities in Spanish & English Book 4	$14.95	
	SPANISH made FUN & EASY Book 1	$14.95	
	SPANISH made FUN & EASY Book 2	$14.95	

Fisher Hill
5267 Warner Ave., #166
Huntington Beach, CA 92649-4079
www.Fisher-Hill.com

Phone
714-377-9353
800-494-4652
Fax
714-377-9495

Add 7.75% for shipments to California addresses.

Add 10% of TOTAL for shipping.

TOTAL _____

SALES TAX _____

SHIPPING _____

PAYMENT _____

BALANCE DUE _____

Fisher Hill books are developed by teachers with Master's degrees in Education and a combined 40 years of teaching experience.
Orders are sent by United Parcel Service. Add 10% of total for shipping.
All products are guaranteed. If you are not happy with an item, send it back for a full refund. All returned materials must be received in perfect condition.